LIGHT TECHNIQUES

THAT TRIGGER

TRANSFORMATION

By VYWAMUS
Through
Janet McClure

Edited By
Lillian Harben

BOOKS BY JANET McCLURE
PUBLISHED BY LIGHT TECHNOLOGY

AHA!
The Realization Book

Light Techniques
That Trigger Transformation

Sanat Kumara
Training a Planetary Logos

Scopes of Dimensions:
How to Experience
Multi-Dimensional Reality

The Source Adventure

Light Techniques
That Trigger Transformation

ISBN NO. 0-929385-00-4

Published by Light Technology Publishing
P.O. Box 3540, Flagstaff, AZ 86003
(520) 526-1345 • (800) 450-0985

INTRODUCTION TO VYWAMUS

Vywamus is a great being, a cosmic being who has come among us to serve during these critical, yet marvelous times when humanity seeks to evolve into spiritual consciousness, casting off the outworn "forms" and moving into a greater light, into the New Age. He tells us that he was invoked by Humanity's desire to evolve and came here, as many spiritual teachers are now doing, to make this transition as painless and smooth as possible, and at as high a vibrational level as possible.

Vywamus is a higher aspect of Sanat Kumara, our planetary Logos who ensouls the earth and all upon it and within it. The earth, in effect, is being held together by his consciousness. Vywamus can be equated to the soul of Sanat Kumara.

Long ago Vywamus chose to express in physical existence and evolved through the physical chain just as humanity on this planet has chosen to do. He evolved on a planet far distant from here but one that was similar to the earth. While in physical existence he was offered the opportunity to be a channel for a very high spiritual teacher. He feels that by thus serving he was able to gain clear perception of the nature of existence and evolving consciousness which enabled him to ascend in his next life. Ascension was accomplished after only 37 incarnations in the physical. Because of the experience of his rapid gain in evolution due to his channeling he encourages his students to learn to channel, not only as a service to bring the spiritual teacher's message to the earth, but to aid their own development.

Now in his great love Vywamus has chosen to aid mankind through dedicated channels such as Janet McClure and he offers his teachings through classes and personal work, as well as through sound, which is one of his specialties.

TABLE OF CONTENTS

Page

Introduction   1

Source Structure   6

Assembling Physical Components   10

Cosmic Day Development   14

Overlay Process To Integrate New Level   23

Triggering Creative Fountains of Light   30

Launching Your Light To The Creative Core   33

Technique For Expanding The Heart Center   42

Mirror Reversal   46

Your Emotional Body Through The   50
Dimensions

Accepting or Integrating The Full Energy Of   58
The Emotional Body

Releasing The Destructive Focus   68

Helping The Emotional Body Use The   71
Third Dimension

i

Sliding Affirmations Into The Lake   78

Releasing Habit Patterns Of The Emotional   81
Body In Dealing With Trauma

Using A Dodecahedron Focus   90

Freeing-Up The 4-Body System In The   92
Dimensions

Energizing And Transcending   96

Energizing The Chakras With A Blue   100
Electrical Star

The "V" Focus   105

Stepping On Light   107

Weaving The Garment Of Light   109

Relating To Mass Consciousness   116

Adding Light To The Body   122

The Golden Ball   125

Energizing Goals By Breaking Up Crystallized   127
Patterns

Finding A Key In The Light   131

Lighting-Up Communication   133

Getting In Touch With The Rhythm Of   134
Existence

Light Alignment   135

Using The Soul To Balance The Physical   139
And Monadic Levels

Electrical Stimulation Of Integration   143

PHYSICAL LEVEL OF ENERGY BODY
CHAKRA DESCRIPTIONS

1. **BASE CHAKRA**
   Survival

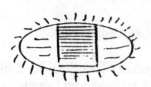

2. **POLARITY CHAKRA**
   Receptive/Dynamic Energies

3. **SOLAR PLEXUS CHAKRA**
   Emotional Center

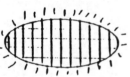

4. **HEART CHAKRA**
   Unconditional Love

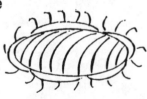

5. **THROAT CHAKRA**
   Creativity/Will

6. THIRD EYE
   Integration of Seeing Process

7. CROWN CHAKRA
   Divine Connection

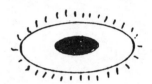

8. SEAT OF THE SOUL

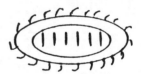

9. BODY OF LIGHT

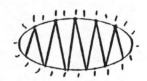

10. POLARITY BALANCE
    Integrates Creativity and Flow

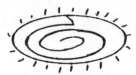

INTRODUCTION

Light technology is an evolving science, truly part
of the New Age. Over the history of the earth light
has been rather misunderstood. In other words,
light has always been sought but what it truly
represented has not yet been comprehended.
Many of you enjoy lying on a beach soaking up the
rays of the sun, your body feels warmed by those
rays and many of you like the way you look when
exposed to light energy. Humanity has always
valued a "tan" at least those of you with skin light
enough to show it. The goal, then, is to
understand light because physical existence could
not exist without it. Plants need light to grow and
human beings react psychologically if deprived of
light for long periods of time. Light is then a key, a
necessity, and in the following material I would like
to explore light in many, many ways.

I am a spiritual teacher, light energy if you will, who
has seen and been inspired to come to the earth
by the light energy of your planet. The earth
radiates a beautiful energy that shows its evolving
understanding, its growth shows the beauty of its
evolving consciousness. Certainly the earth is set
solidly, at least it has been, in the third dimension
but through the process of evolution it approaches
the fourth dimension and thus has awakened
responses from the fourth dimensional perspective
which are now adding light energy to it. If you are
baking a cake and you add egg whites that have
been beaten up and are very fluffy to your cake, if
you fold in those egg whites the cake becomes

1

lighter. You can see from this example how much lighter the earth's perspective is becoming by adding the egg whites analogy which in this example represents the light energy. This light energy needs to be added carefully so that its effervescence is distributed in a way that can enhance the qualities of the earth which have already been placed in a very positive perspective. What I mean by that is, the earth has learned a great deal, although, one may sense there is more to learn. There is a basic level of learning which has already been accepted that transcends anything else ever before within the history of your planet and this includes that light civilization called Egypt. Many of you are beginning to utilize abilities that you used in Egypt. You see these abilities or allow them to light up your life now thus this lighting up process allows the strengths that you have already used and understood to be the means by which your evolution takes place and also the earth's.

Light is important then because it points out strengths which transcend points that seem stuck or a perspective of life that is not desired allowing the life through this strength or light energy to become a more balanced, a more integrated, more allowing, more receptive point of view. To receive one must give, but light is the carrier of receptivity and it cannot evolve until the receptivity area is lit up, until your heart is acknowledged as the means to light up the way to create your life and your part of the Creator's plan for the earth.

I have attempted in this book to stretch you conceptually and there are some quite conceptual areas. Please read them allowing them to stretch you even if reading it the first time all of what I am telling you may not yet be completely understood. You will be able to glimpse components of light in a step by step manner through studying this material and then gradually you will be able to fit them altogether until there is an integrated understanding within you of what light energy is and this perhaps is the most important part of this book. I have given you many, many exercises in order that you may explore and experience light energy in a conscious manner. These techniques can be the bridge that unifies your understanding of light creating a radiating point which then encompasses a whole area allowing you to take one more step in your understanding.

I would suggest that you read through this material once, from cover to cover. You may then wish to take it apart selecting certain exercises that you wish to try and then going back to the broad overview and specifics given in regard to light and studying them.

Use the diagrams as a visual means of establishing contact with an archetypal or blueprinting point. If you study something conceptually and visualize or light up the energy in a visual manner you can unify the four body system in its understanding. The mental body views the concept, the emotional body flows through the light symbol which is spiritual in nature into locking-in the understanding into a physical foundation which can guide your life. This is done in as comprehensive a manner as you allow. For many of you, each time you relate and discover through a light exercise a way to unite the conceptual, emotional, spiritual and physical you will have lit up a possibility that can then transcend in your life in a very practical manner those areas which have seemed difficult or not yet clear. This book then is a very practical tool in using light to transcend because it has lit up a clearer perspective. Those areas, that have over and over again been heavily energized or caught into a perspective that seems stuck can be lit up. When you turn the light on in a closet you can see what you've stored there. Many times that simple act of turning on the light will show you how to use your closet in a practical manner, the closet being the storage system by which you create your life. You may want to clean out your closet once in a while but as long as the light is on there, you can use it even if there is yet some cleaning out to do. You can use it in a manner that has you transcending some of the material that is still stored there in the closet but you haven't yet released. One of these days you will go into your closet and say "it's time to give away what I am not using there." In an energy sense then you will gather up what you no longer need in your closet, take it out, and return it to the cosmos so this energy can be re-used, re-cycled if you will.

I invite you then to come with me on this journey of light, be patient with yourself as you discover, as you allow yourself to receive in a comprehensive manner the symbols given, through the written

4

word - the concepts, through the visual symbols -
the diagrams, and through the exercises given to
you. This truly is a journey of light, let us together
light up the cosmos through your clearer
understanding.

Vywamus

(speaking for those of us who have journeyed just
a step or two further along the light path.)

SOURCE STRUCTURE

The Source explores through what we might term a structural flow. As a river flows there is a structure called a riverbed which supports that flow. The Source's structure contains many different, what one might term, identifiable structures that we may look at to understand what it is that is being symbolized. This material is meant to explore in many ways the structural flow of Source, giving diagrams and techniques to aid in the understanding of it's structure.

Now, it is structure that conveys the basic beingness of the Source and as it flows it communicates with itself, with other points of view or other structures, and as it interacts light is created. It takes the movement of the structure interacting on many levels and within many perspectives to create light. We seek then to grow - to gain a further understanding of what light is and how to understand its unlimited nature, of how then to access through such an understanding our own unlimited nature. We will begin by giving you some diagrams which identify certain symbols and how to use these symbols to gain a basic awareness of light interaction. Remember the structure conveys the light. It is the vehicle that utilizes the energy including the visible portion of the energy, which is light.

Diagram #1 then shows you three structures. At the top is a circle. Within that circle are fifteen smaller circles. Because this is a multi-dimensional structure we see the fifteen circles as

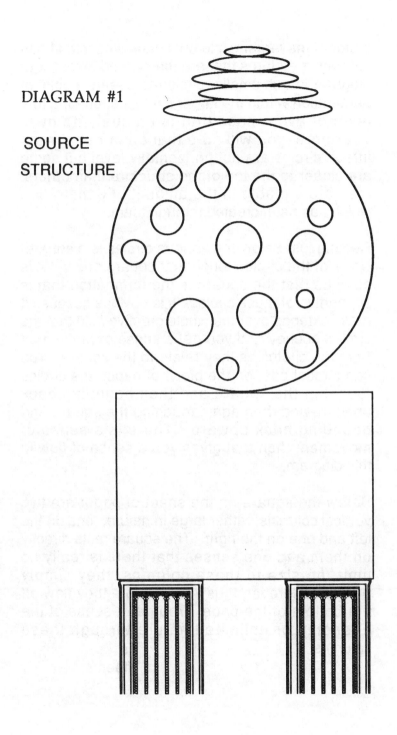

DIAGRAM #1

SOURCE
STRUCTURE

a part of the larger circle but connecting into fifteen different structures that are the second level of our diagram. Each smaller circle represents a point of penetration within the larger circle, penetrating to a level of awareness that is uniquely its own. Therefore, you will note that on our paper the fifteen circles are not horizontally level but some are closer to the top of the structure than others; they are variable in the amount of penetration which has been created through them.

Resting just below the various circles is a square. None of the circles touch that square and yet it is obvious that the square is the foundation that is supportive of these circles. It is obvious because it really extends over the whole creative field that the circles occupy and you get a sense of movement from the circles as they relate to the square. You can almost see, on the piece of paper, the circles touching the square and then bounding back upward, and then again touching the square and bounding back upward. There is a sense of movement then that gives you a sense of flow in this diagram.

Below the square on the sheet of paper are two vertical columns, rather large in nature, one on the left and one on the right. The square rests directly on them and one senses that there is really no limit, no size to these columns, they simply penetrate forever, thus you will note they flow off the bottom of the page. You get a sense of the unending or unlimited nature through these columns.

Look then at the overall nature of this diagram. The square is physical existence, the circle is the whole perspective on the spiritual level. The smaller circles are points of view which are being penetrated within, through physical existence, in order to understand clearly what that larger circle means. The two columns are the polarity of existence and you can gain a sense of motion from this diagram which instead of putting physical existence as a by-product of creation shows clearly that a penetration to it and a movement and contact with it keep creating a Source level motion or increased understanding of what we have termed evolution.

Above the circle you will see a light spiral. Literally as the smaller circles keep interacting with physical existence that spiral light grows and divine movement or evolution takes place. Truly that's the only kind of motion that exists - the evolutionary process. All other motion on the physical level is simply a penetration which takes apart the creative process through sequential time and space so that one may understand the process and how to utilize it in an integrated manner. You could say that each time one of those small circles touches physical existence a light stimulus occurs which allows the movement or flow of the light in a manner that is represented by the next diagram.

As you will note, this Diagram #1, contains squares, circles, straight lines and other combinations of basic creative connections. It shows through this creative symbolism the

8

stimulus to the creative principle itself which comes through physical existence. I mean to convey here, then, that the vehicle for creating more light, which is called physical existence produces a certain type of creativity and we can view it visually.

At other levels, another type of creativity is produced. Perhaps the best way to give you an example here, beyond the visual drawing, would be to say that a flute when played, produces certain vibrational tones. If you play a cello or a piano or a harp you get a different framework or different structure through which to produce the vibrational pattern and thus what is produced has a different structure in its creative foundation.

ASSEMBLING PHYSICAL COMPONENTS

I give you here then, in Diagram #2 the creative result of using physical existence which inputs to the Source and allows a structural increase which becomes a magnet drawing into it from other levels which have not been physical components. They were created spiritually but have not yet been, what one might term, locked into the creative process. Think about a house that is being built - some of it is pre-fabricated. You have, then, lying around, walls with window frames, you have other pieces of the structure but they are just lying around - partially constructed. First then, one puts up a foundation which we could call the creative input brought to the point that has been prepared for it at the Source level. The physical plane then creates a vibrational effect which is a foundation into which all partially assembled creative components can fit.

Now, keep in mind that we are talking about creation from one point of view, this cosmic day, this conceptual exploration. There have been cosmic days that had no physical component thus the creative basis was different but in this cosmic day the creative effect that physical existence brings to the basic level is used to create that foundation that attracts certain rather elusive creative principles that have not yet been integrated. This is important because it shows that on a cosmic day it takes some sequential time in physical existence to construct an understanding on the physical plane that is radiant and magnetic enough to invoke those specific, rather elusive partially constructed components which will help it to complete the conceptual frameworking system that the Source is constructing. Diagram #2 shows you the creative foundation which is beginning to be radiant and invocative enough to attract the creative components which will complete it.

Diagram #3 shows an enlargement of the component that is being attracted by Diagram #2. I show it in quite a lot of detail so that you may see its structure, and in a symbolic sense, be able to refer to its size relationship, if you will. You can see the much greater volume of creativity brought by physical existence but the fine and delicate nature of the component which is being attracted to this foundation. There are many such components that simply are awaiting the invocative process which is now available in this cosmic day from the resonating quality that all of physical existence is beginning to manifest. Manifestation, then, is for the purpose of resonating a creative principle strongly enough that it will attract all of the creative points required to be used in evolving the creative principle that is being manifested.

The third diagram shows you how the creative foundation which, remember, is the creative effect brought through physical existence, locks into the creative component being attracted to it through the invocative contact between them. Look closely at where the two are coming together and you will note certain lines that are of the female and male principle. Although the physical effect is doing the invoking, it is acting as the female, or receptive, and the spiritual component being drawn to it is the

DIAGRAM #2

ATTRACTING A NEW PHYSICAL COMPONENT

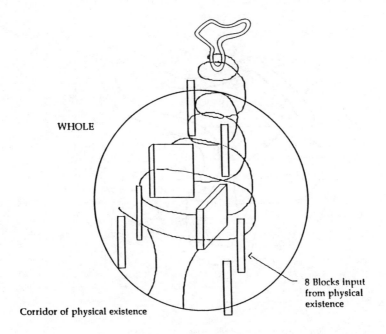

WHOLE

Corridor of physical existence

8 Blocks input
from physical
existence

DIAGRAM #3

ENLARGEMENT OF COMPONENT ATTRACTED IN DIAGRAM #2

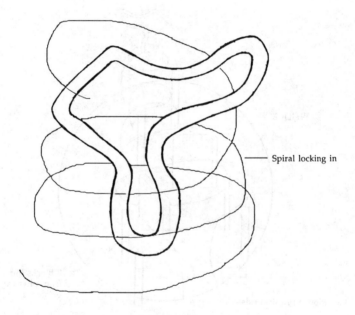

———— Spiral locking in

Example of the male principal component. This shape is
one of 7 possibilities.

male or dynamic principle locking into this receptor. The drawing indicates the receptive and dynamic principle as given.

It is necessary, in order to use this material, to let go of preconceived notions about how creativity takes place. Some of you have not been aware that there is divine structure. You do understand that there is flow. Flow is always contained in a divine sense, in an ideal sense. The containment is the supportive nature of the Whole as it supports or allows the flow to be present in its evolution. Look again at the diagram where the two components are coming together. As the spiritual thrust settles in, is received, by the foundation built for it, as the two contact each other there is an expansion of light. This creative expansion unifies the creative principle joining both points of view and thus this aspect of creativity becomes more complete within the Whole's growing awareness or exploration of this particular creative principle. Remember, one must stretch and allow the conceptual view of unlimitedness to see, at least a little, what I am seeking to convey. There is always an expanded point of view and the mechanics of that expanded point of view are what we are looking at in these diagrams. We are also saying that physical existence contains for the creative principle an important foundation which is invocative of points of view that are seeking to be assimilated but need that particular foundation in order to be so assimilated.

The next diagram, Diagram #4, shows that the light expansion pattern gained as a major component is

DIAGRAM #4

LIGHT EXPANSION PATTERN OF COMPONENT

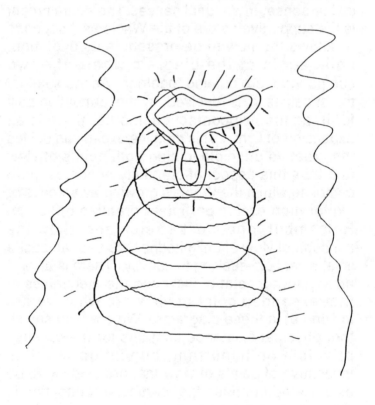

locked-in to the foundation that physical existence has created and has been brought into a basic spiritual premise as shown in the previous diagrams.

COSMIC DAY DEVELOPMENT

I would like to give you now some diagrams which show a cosmic day and its development. Because each cosmic day, which, remember, is a conceptual framework with a theme, is created a little differently, we will look at the construction of this cosmic day whose theme is courage.

Now I, Vywamus, can give you the constructural framework in a manner that will allow your creativity to view it. That is why I am using these diagrams and these symbols, your subconscious mind understands beyond your mental or emotional expression what is being given here. Thus, assimilating the material given here will allow you to understand and perhaps bridge to an opening in the use of symbols which will stretch your higher mental opening and begin for you a much wider use of that higher mental or conceptual body area. This is the purpose for studying this material. Certainly it may be interesting - I hope so, but beyond that it is transformational, creating openings through which you can sense divine structures - growth, how it fits together, and how a lightening perspective of the Source really occurs.

Diagram 5A in this cosmic day series shows a basic premise coming forth. Diagram 5B shows about 1/4 through the cosmic day, Diagram 5C about half and Diagram 5D about three-quarters and Diagram 5E the completion of our cosmic day on courage. Take a look at the locking-in principle utilized at our current point of evolution which is

DIAGRAM 5A
Cosmic Day
Basic Premise

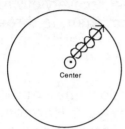

DIAGRAM 5B
1/4 Cosmic Day

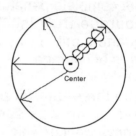

DIAGRAM 5C
1/2 Cosmic Day

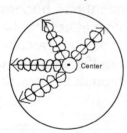

DIAGRAM 5D
3/4 Cosmic Day

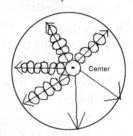

DIAGRAM 5 E
Cosmic Day Completion

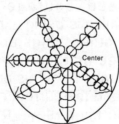

approximately three-quarters of the way through this cosmic day. We must note that only a small percentage of the perspective of this cosmic day is sequential, only that within physical existence, which is about one-tenth of the Whole but mostly we are talking about the allowing by the Source of the complete penetration into the discovery of what courage truly is. The Source, then, is three-quarters of the way in its creative excursion in the area of courage.

The three-quarter point is a critical one. And its beginning was symbolized by your Harmonic Convergence, which was a time of the locking-in of several of these creative components I discussed earlier. In other words, at this point, the one-tenth of existence that is called physical has become able to create or produce a creative effect that has locked-in at the basic level a radiant and invocative effect allowing much in the area of the structure of what courage is to be received through the locking-in process.

You might think about courage. It has many facets, does it not? Certainly on the earth you can see how, indeed, courage is a very basic characteristic which is being explored. You might say that many other things are being explored also, and I agree that there have been about a million cosmic days from this point of view of the Source alone, and the current exploration comes through, or you might say - the creative effort contains points of view or what we have called beliefs from all of the explorations that have been made in the past. In other words, at Source level also is a mass-consciousness and this mass-consciousness is the storage system, the creative vehicle of all that has been. Thus if you explore courage, you look at everything else that has already been explored and learn about courage through what has been. The goal, of course, is to keep what serves you well in the area of what has been and to let go of what does not, and the Source, in its clarity, is able to do this On its level, everything that is has experienced is absolutely clear because it does not retain or keep anything that is not.

In a personal sense, each of us is learning also to be that clear in applying the creative principle. Thus, as the components of creativity are locked-in through a radiant and invocative effect produced by physical existence there is a very important shifting, enlarging, spiraling, literally almost what one might call a creative explosion that is occurring now. Now, not in a irritative sense, not at the level of the Source. In a personal sense the irritative quality may be there and that must be released, but in an expanding sense that creative explosion creates light of such magnitude that it is certainly awesome to view. Also the explosion keeps making available - literally - the tenfold expansion of its creativity factors through each of these creative explosions. Every time one of them occurs the Source's understanding grows in a proportion that is tenfold to what it has been. It expands then, ten times what it has been, as an example. It is necessary to apply that principle to our diagrams, to understand the nature of what is currently occurring in this cosmic day. Certainly in a spiritual sense, but for many of you, from a practical point of view, this is what is occurring now on the earth

I give you one cross in Diagram #6 and into that cross comes an arrow. See that coming in. Where the arrow touches the crossed point of the cross there is a creative explosion and in Diagram #6B you will see a larger cross, the arrow is gone and surrounding it are ten other crosses of equal magnitude, equal creativity, equal understanding. Thus, the creative principle has multiplied itself as the arrow, the dynamic flow, touched its critical mass point, or that point of sensitivity which balanced its creative output and allowed a sense of unity and understanding that expanded it in every direction. Indeed, that is what you as a creator are looking for - the center where the lines cross, that sensitive point which allows an equality of input to the creative principle. Because the creative input which is allowed then expands the creative output which is a resultant factor of accepting an equality of creative input. You might consider that now.

Seek to recognize then, that each time this resultant factor, brought through physical existence, invokes a creative component which is locked-in that the creativity level of the Whole is multiplied. What that means to you now on the physical level is that your creativity has been multiplied and your potential literally made ten times greater through the harmonic convergence. A little effort produces ten-times as much result. Also, there is a need to be sure that you want what

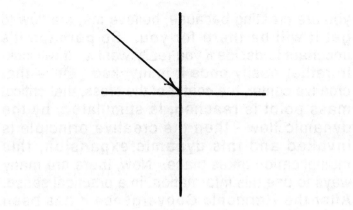

DIAGRAM 6B

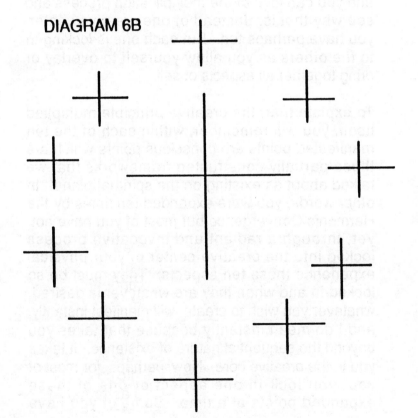

you are creating because, believe me, the flow to get it will be there for you. So perhaps it's important to decide if you really want it. It will lock-in rather easily once it is invoked. Once that creative center, the center of the cross, that critical mass point is reached, is stimulated, by the dynamic flow - then the creative principle is invoked and this dynamic expansion, this multiplication takes place. Now, there are many ways to use this information, in a practical sense. After the Harmonic Convergence it has been difficult for humanity to find their creative center and you can look at the multiplication process and see why that is. Instead of one creative center, you have perhaps ten. But each one is locking-in to the others as you allow yourself to overlay or bring together all aspects of self.

To explain that; the creative principle multiplied itself, you will remember, within each of the ten manifested points are conscious points which are those partially constructed frameworks that we talked about as existing on the spiritual plane. In other words, you were expanded ten times by the Harmonic Convergence but most of you have not, yet, through a radiant and invocative process locked into the creative center of your physical experience these ten aspects. They must be so locked-in and when they are whatever is desired, whatever you wish to create, will manifest instantly, and I do mean instantly because that takes you beyond the sequential nature of existence. It takes you to the creative core. Now, perhaps, for most of you, you lock-in one aspect or one of these expanded points at a time. Some of you have locked-in several already. The key is allowing the receptivity of the creative principle, knowing that the male and female principle will be the process through which the overlaying of all of the levels which the expansion represents come together. Know then, that you will know as these expanded points come together just as you recognize someone that you've known over and over again from the past - they are familiar and you are comfortable with them and you communicate well with them generally speaking. There is a familiarity about them. Thus as you bring your creative components back together in a conscious manner after the expanded awareness of the Whole has ignited them you will recognize or realize they are coming together because they are familiar parts and they know each other well.

The most important part as far as I could see is to recognize what is occurring and once you've seen this multiplying process and recognize the creative principle within which you are evolving you can be more allowing with the time that it takes to put everything back together again. The problem for most of you has been in not knowing what has been occurring. Thus as this is a joint authorship between Vywamus and Lenduce we have put together some material to help you directly, through symbols and structure to access your creativity .

By the time you read this book you probably will have realized the importance of the Harmonic Convergence but let me show you in another Diagram #7A how important I think it is. I give you

DIAGRAM #7

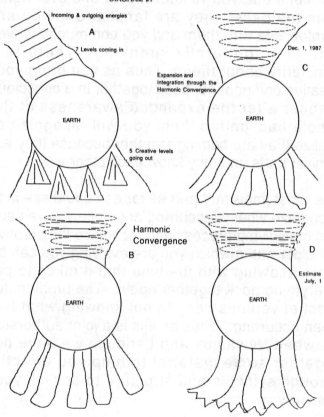

A
Incoming & outgoing energies

7 Levels coming in

Expansion and
integration through the
Harmonic Convergence

EARTH

5 Creative levels
going out

C
Dec. 1, 1987

EARTH

Harmonic
Convergence

B

EARTH

D
Estimate
July, 1

EARTH

then, the earth as a ball and the incoming and outgoing energy patterns in a rather simple manner from before the Convergence. You will note the energy interchange as being definite but not all encompassing. Note the next Diagram #7B and what occurred in the energy patterns, both within the earth and into the earth at the time of the Convergence. The date is August 17th, 1987. I give you in the third Diagram #7C, December 1, 1987; and in the final Diagram #7D, my estimate of what it would be like at the end of July, 1988. July is a very important month here on your earth. Plus by the end of it some important structural changes will have occurred as far as energy and the expansion of the creative process is concerned.

Note then, the progression of what one might call the communication changes between the incoming and outgoing energies on your earth. It seems more complicated now doesn't it? It really isn't but there is a great deal more input and output because the creative level has been multiplied tenfold. It is important then to allow the earth's changes to be also within you. You are, then, an aspect of the earth's expansion and within your personal evolution you also have multiplied tenfold your creative effort. This may be difficult to grasp from your current life perspective. Certainly, I am not saying that all of you have yet been able to create ten times as clearly as before, however, that creative opening is present, the multiplication has taken place, all that remains to be done and I mean ALL that remains to be done is to overlay again each multiple component so that it fits together consciously and from a clear choice level into this larger framework of creativity.

You see, a universal law is free will on every level, so in the final analysis, every aspect on every level must choose clearly to integrate into the larger perspective. Some, you might say, drag their heels a little, confusing the area of freedom, not recognizing that true freedom comes through surrendering to this greater process, that the only way to be free is to be a component of the Whole that allows an unlimited expression. Each aspect of you then must choose to overlay with every other aspect into a creative centering that when completely equalized is the creative base that is your unlimited expression.

An alignment process is occurring within each of you. In the previous material we talked about the multiplying process and having now to overlay ten aspects into a creative foundation which has now been created. Let us in a step by step manner give you some techniques to use in gaining an understanding of what is occurring and to assist you in facilitating the process.

First of all, then, remember the Harmonic Convergence allowed that creative base to come forth on the earth so it is through your earth relationship that you can most clearly access that basic creativity foundation you are seeking. This is so important that I advise you to seek to be aware of your earth relationship at all times. Some of you have sought to leave the earth or rather reluctantly view yourself as a part of it. Believe me, at this point, in your awareness, in your growth, the earth is your friend. The divine structure of the earth is clearly invocative of the contact points you are seeking to integrate within your own system and I would encourage you to look at your own divine connection through that divine connection of the earth. Let me give you a technique and another diagram as we discuss it.

See the earth as a ball. It simply has been given as an energy focus. Now sense this focus, this energy, from a whole point of view, don't try to take it apart, seeing certain geographical areas or people or plants or animals or the crust of the earth itself. Simply as a focus that has all of the components of the earth within it. Sit and come in contact with that energy, allow it literally to permeate your physical structure and your energy structure. It will, you know, when you invoke it. That whole perspective will come into you. Now remember, the earth is a reflection of the Source itself and as you allow that whole to come into your physical body, you are literally invoking a perspective of wholeness that is then the foundation that you are seeking to begin to use in your overlaying system.

OVERLAY PROCESS TO INTEGRATE NEW LEVEL

Now, let us say that we have eleven sheets of paper, the basic or foundation one is opaque, it is a beautiful green, an emerald green. The other ten are transparent and they are various colors. It doesn't really matter which is what but you have all colors coming in. There's a pink one and a red one and a yellow one and a violet and an orange and blue and various combinations of colors, silver and gold and white. All colors, but they are transparent. These are the ten aspects that will be overlayed onto the green opaque one that is your earth relationship, your foundation.

Now, with your knowingness, I would like you to select a color. Whatever one your knowingness selects and see that overlayed onto the green, the foundation. Now, as that overlay occurs, ask your creativity what that color represents and write it down. You have ten overlays and I want you to get ten different aspects. Now they will not be the same for all of you but let me give you some possibilities. Certainly, there is the love center. There is the spiritual body, the mental, the emotional and the physical bodies themselves. There is the polarity areas - the female and the male polarities. There is the will center, there is the creative or subconscious center. There is the evolutionary process itself and your relationship to it. There is freedom of choice area which is a little different than the will center, although, for some of you, you will use them together. There are then, choices to be made - what colors will represent what aspects.

Base color is Green

COLORS	ASPECTS
RED	Earth Relationship
ORANGE	Spiritual Body
YELLOW	Emotional Body
BLUE	Physical Body
PURPLE	Mental Body
VIOLET	Male Polarity
PINK	Female Polarity
SILVER	Conceptual Area
GOLD	Subconscious or Creative Center
WHITE	Love Center
	Third Eye
	Will Center
	Freedom of Choice
	Evolutionary Process
	Space Relationship
	Dimensional Relationship
	Electrical Relationship
	Rhythmic Relationship
	Light Relationship
	Other "far out" Relationship

Use your knowingness or intuition to select an aspect from the column on the right to go with each color listed in the column on the left. You are choosing on the basis of the amount of energy in this aspect and the kind of energy as symbolized by the color.

First of all, then, place one color sheet over the green, find out what it represents - write that down on a slip of paper and then take that one off - put on another one and ask what that represents and write that down on a slip of paper until you get your ten. If you do not have a light box and colored foils or sheets you can visualize the color lit up. Now, there really are ten. If you get less or more, do again a little bit of evaluation because you may be doubling or missing something that can be very important. Some of you may have some "far out" perceptions. Maybe it will be your space relationship that's important as one of these. It may be, perhaps, your dimensional relationship as one of the ten, or your electrical relationship, or your rhythmic relationship or your light relationship. You see, the ten are going to be different for each one of you but I'd like you to use your knowingness to get the color and the perspective. Now, after you have written down all ten, then again, using your knowingness, list them, the ten, in the order in which the overlay should be done for you. It will be different for each of you. For many of you, perhaps for most of you, the conceptual area and the heart area, the emotional body and the choice areas are key ingredients. Some of you then, have other priorities, but for all of you these are important.

Now I would suggest that you either work with a friend who can literally embody these aspects for you or, if you prefer, you create an internal dialogue with them, visualizing each aspect as a person. In other words, let us say that you get the color pink, for the heart, and that is the first area that comes up that needs to be overlayed into your new creative base. Then personify or see your heart as a person. Now, as you attempt to get in touch with it you may ask a friend "Will you tune in with your knowingness and bring me what you receive in regard to what I need to do to have my heart area more an integrated part of me?" Your friend will tune in then, or you will tune in then if you are doing it yourself and you will get specific points which can be resolved so that you will be more conscious of the opportunity to use the love center in an integrated manner.

Now, because the heart is quite complex, it may be broken down - certain aspects of the heart are; trust, receptivity, allowingness, humility, gratitude, etc. You may, if you wish, continue to personify in this breaking down process, aspects of the heart. Perhaps when you try to trust there is a betrayal of your trust. You may wish, in a regression, to look at certain times when your trust seemed violated. By doing so you begin to process or bring into a more integrated space this aspect of the heart center and as you realize more clearly what the heart center is and how to use it you can allow the overlaying process to take place. It probably will be necessary to keep working on these aspects, in other words, I think most of you will realize that you will continue to develop your understanding of the heart or the love center. You reach certain plateaus which are then integrated and then you continue to discover more. Allow your awareness to include now this next step for you in the overlaying system. What is it that is being overlayed? You've expanded tenfold your abilities but now what is it that is necessary to bring those abilities into an aligned point of sensitivity where they can create for you a balanced life. This exercise can be expanded until you have gone through all ten overlays. Now, when you feel, and only then - my friend - you have gained some understanding of all ten, then I would suggest a visualization where you visualize the opaque green and then you overlay in the order that you feel is important, each one of the ten.

You see, the goal is this: to consciously overlay until a point of synthesis is created where again that expansive, what we have called explosion, takes place which then locks-in the new level that is available and makes available an integrative use of the old level. What I didn't discuss before is that also what occurred in the Harmonic Convergence is a locking-in of the creative process, the productive part of it on the earth, and a completeness that is very satisfying as you view it. Things are complete in a way that they were not before. You can view them as complete. You will begin to see that completeness here on your earth.

Now, that doesn't mean that on the earth level the view of the completeness is absolutely clear, but what I am telling you is that before there didn't seem to be any pieces to fit in to many situations. Now, from this level of creativity that has been completed, all of the pieces are there and are easily, at least rather easily, accessed on the human level. It is the new level that has been expanded into that is not yet manifesting the use of all of it's pieces. You can't see that on the new level yet but on the level that is now complete, you can.

27

Going back and looking at your life as it has been before will be extremely helpful in this regard. Now as you overlay then, all ten, onto the opaque green, sense or seek a point of synthesis, a point of blending. Now make no mistake, when it goes to a major new level you will know it. You will absolutely know it. There is no way to mistake this creative point but for a while some synthesis will take place and it may be that you can't always tell if anything has been accomplished through your overlaying but keep at it and also keep looking at each aspect because when each aspect is clear enough and there are no major points of resistance then it will all fit together in an invocative manner that then, remember - both locks in a new level - multiplies your creativity and we might say also makes available a completeness of what has been gained.

This is an exciting concept. I hope that you will use this often in your exploration of who you are. It is necessary, of course, to be honest with yourself. If there is difficulty in the will area, if surrender to the plan seems difficult, then you don't "hit yourself over the head" with this area but you recognize there is some resistance there yet and you seek to discover why. Regression to a past life or the personification of an aspect by someone else can be very helpful in seeing why you have created this area that is yet resistive to the integrative or overlaying process. Make no mistake - you truly do create everything in your life and because of that you can now create everything that you want as long as you keep utilizing a process of penetration in order to reach that new creative

base. You might look again at Diagram #1 with the larger circles and the smaller circles. Each penetration that resounds onto the physical plane allows a clearer expression of that whole point of view that is being explored. So thus, the deeper you go into your understanding in each of the aspects the sooner will come about a balance of the overlay which allows your expanded point of view to come forth.

TRIGGERING CREATIVE FOUNTAINS OF LIGHT

Now because you are not alone in the universe, there are beings literally at every point of consciousness. In other words, you are surrounded by the creativity or you might say the light of the Whole. Because it is really a joint effort - the creation of the Whole - there are ways to invoke the light contact point that will bring forth a surge of energy or what one might call creative power.

Truly my subject, light, is the key to understanding how to create in a clear manner. Although you may know this with your mental body we wish to demonstrate the persuasiveness that light can lead to the full acceptance of the next step in your evolution or the putting together of a surge of creativity that is much more comprehensive than you thought possible. It is an exciting concept to see how light truly triggers creativity. Now think about that word - triggers - I've been talking about it lately. This volume is really being offered by Lenduce and I together and when we say "trigger" we mean a point that comes together in creativity and through the interaction at that point of creativity launches the creativity to a more comprehensive point of awareness or consciousness or expansion. There is literally a movement of the creativity and divine movement is simply an expansion of consciousness - that's the difference between movement on the physical plane and movement on the spiritual level. Yes, there is movement but it is not sequential. It is expansive of the awareness level whether it is the Whole we are speaking of or a developing being within that Whole perspective such as you are.

Thus, there are a number of ways to "trigger" this expansion through integrative techniques. First you integrate and then through the strength that the integrating represents expansion comes forth. We could say that there is a layering of energy or abilities into an integrative point. You keep putting things in and an emphasis is made then at that point. Because of the emphasis there is strength gained or more energy placed within a creative point and the expansion is possible then through an acceptance by self. The acknowledgement of that integrative point begins the triggering process that then effectively launches the creativity into an expansive state.

Now, because of that, one must be able to choose the use of the integrated space. For instance, if you go to a dance you must choose to dance if you wish to utilize the opportunity that the dance environment brings to you. You can sit on the sidelines and if you do you may enjoy it but you will not experience the expansion that is available through what the dance opportunity brings to you. Now on the physical level it may be that the dance is simply an enjoyment that brings you in contact with others and that is enough of a motive on any level. Enjoyment is important and it is a major awareness in itself that life is enjoyable. In my opinion the reason why the Source itself has manifested is enjoyment, is the love of the expansive awareness of what beingness is and the use of techniques on every level are simply in relationship to the Source's desire and love and enjoyment of the expansive awareness of all possibilities. Thus, we are all a part of this expansive process in the manifested state. Perhaps later in this material but certainly in other materials I would like to go deeper into that concept of the non-manifested state and help you to see the point that is behind non-manifestation and the delicate nature of building a bridge to the manifested state. But that is, perhaps, not our subject right now.

In manifestation then, the goal is, and yes it is my friends - an expansion, a total expansion and by that I mean expanding everything that becomes available for expansion and because it is an eternal process that means everything from every point of view, on every level. Now perhaps in order to appreciate the expansive process we choose to expand a particular point of awareness by triggering that expansion process. We do this with a light trigger that holds that point of consciousness that has been triggered as a center, a magnetic center that then radiates light out to a comprehensive radiating field that allows a penetration of the creativity into areas that have not yet been explored, acknowledged or understood. The creative explosive nature of the triggering process brings an alignment with the creative core of Source allowing that radiating field to be both magnified and magnetized in a creative sense.

LAUNCHING YOUR LIGHT TO THE CREATIVE CORE

Look at it this way - let us say that we have a beautiful divine device that is rather like a rocket launcher and it has an ability to launch what has been placed within it very rapidly into a particular creative core. Now the target is gold and this gold is a creative core that you are attempting to reach but perhaps in your understanding you have not yet seen how to reach it. Let us say that this gold - this creative core - represents an understanding in the love area, an integrative understanding of the possibilities of loving unconditionally and being loved in turn unconditionally. All right, now your goal is to literally go to that creative core in the unconditional love area and now we have a launching device that launches a particular unit of consciousness within you. This point that is being launched is the light that you have gained in your present understanding in the love area. Your divine intent or your desire to create in line with the plan or your need to serve others as well as self becomes the means to launch your understanding beyond the current light level. Whatever your present strengths are in the love area can launch you to this new understanding.

Now, light is really the interactive part of vibration, the part that comes through the energy flow as it comes in contact with other parts of the Whole. Thus light is a radiant and invocative projectile to launch into the core of a clearer creative point of view. You also allow this light of your present understanding to become a radiant point that will literally say to the Whole, "I wish to understand the love area in an unlimited manner and I now invoke it through this light contact point." It becomes first a projectile that goes into the center, the core, and then an invocative point through its light radiating qualities. The magnetic core of the Whole, when penetrated by a light projectile, invokes into itself all points of view or the energy that is constantly a part of the mechanism of the Source's expansion. You see, there is a radiating core of understanding that is invocative. The means to evolve the Whole or the Source's understanding is the energy that is attracted by means of contacting this electrical magnetic core. This core is then stimulative, both to the expansion process and the invocative process that brings in the energy or the life force as the means to expand the understanding.

What we are talking about is the way that consciousness expands and if you have a clear understanding of the techniques that can be used in line with the way expansion takes place you can consciously direct your own creative expansion at those particular points where you have gained an integrative understanding - things have come together for you. Now you can use your integrated understanding as a seed thought or projectile that can be launched to the creative core. It is a light projectile that goes into the creative center and begins the expanding process of your Source level understanding.

In other words, the creative core of the Whole is your consciousness at a specific rate of vibration and it is ever becoming more attuned to the vibrational core's basic guiding system. This is because as you, in your unfolding creativity, light up the understandings that show you your true creative potentiality you harmonize your vibration or you become compatible, or your vibratory rate locks into this creative core. You remember earlier we talked about locking-in various aspects of your potential into a foundation of the physical plane. Well, if we look at this process from the Creator's point of view there is a foundation that is invocative and is locking-in all of its creative potential and you are one of those creative potentials that is being locked-in to this creative core. Now, we can look at that in many ways. You are the one that is also, on a new level understanding as a creator doing your own locking-in, but you fit into a larger perspective of the Whole's - the Creator's - effort also and are ever seeking to align or to vibrate your understanding at that very basic level that I am calling the creative core. You can use your understanding that there is such a creative core and then use a light projectile of an integrative point that your understanding has reached to penetrate or go to that creative core and use it's magnetic and radiating strengths to overlay your creativity into the larger system so that the previous techniques that I gave you earlier have a much more widely invocative and radiating space within which to function.

Let me give you the following example: let us say, as we talked about the creative core before, that you have this foundation of understanding built on the physical plane. You also have then in a reflective manner at the Source level a contact point into the radiating foundation of the Whole. Now, one fits into the other, they lock together, they are compatible vibrationally. The way they remain together is from a magnetic invocative vibration which forms a creative chain effect through light triggering techniques. In other words, there is always a creative point within you that is seeking to be launched to the creative core. It carries with it, as it is launched, a thread of light energy that then makes a permanent connection into the creative core of the Source. It means that from that point forever on you have locked-in a particular creative understanding into the larger picture of the Source's level of creativity. Now, it is important to recognize that you have an unlimited number of points that can be launched into the creative core.

Look again at the golden circle that I gave you as an example of the target of reaching the creative core. Now, you will notice that that creative core, that circle, is unlimited. It is. You can look at it as having a particular size but you are looking at it now in the third dimension and if we go beyond the third dimension and place it into the fourth dimension, simply see it becoming a river and you can look at that river at any particular point but it is flowing inter-dimensionally upon a flow that is fourth dimensional in nature but unlimited in its potential. So this creative core, when we take it out of the third dimensional understanding - stretch it into the fourth dimension and then use the strengths of the fifth dimension which is the divine structure that has been manifested on this cosmic day we get a sense of an understanding of the core's creative potential - its creative support system. We also see the way or means the Source has of unlocking its understanding that it already has but has not utilized as a radiant magnetic flow which creates this expansive and exciting creative sense of being.

Now, let me give you the following example. You have in your house a beautiful stereo and it has speakers of the highest quality and you have either records or tapes, that you can play on this machine, but let us say you live in your house for five years and because you are very busy, you don't play that machine. Then one day a friend says to you "Do you ever use your stereo?" And you say "No, I'm really very busy - I have all of these other things that I'm doing, I don't use it." And your friend says "Well, you have a superb sound system that gives you an unlimited perspective of sound. I know because I have this same system." So you say, "Yes, I really haven't used this have I?" And you put on a particular piece of music, one that you haven't heard before - its new, a brand new piece of music to you. You put it on and you sit in that room with your friend, and the music is awesome, the sound literally surrounds you and you sense an expansion of what sound can be itself and you explore through this vibration, this sound state of being that you had not recognized that you had before. That does not mean you didn't have it, but it means that you hadn't explored it through a particular vibration, or a combination of vibrations truly. Your creativity had not activated that sound and explored it.

This is what I am talking about then with our Source. There are many, many levels of Source merging and growing, expanding and yes - triggering creative fountains that spring forth but the Source is ever going into a new room and putting on a combination of vibrations that it has never used before and getting in touch with its creativity from that point of view that it has never expressed before. It has then, virtually, an unlimited number of such rooms and such means to connect into a creative core. You can visualize it by going back now to our fourth dimensional image of your river. Think about a river and how many points, let's say dots - as big as the head of a pin - there are within the flow of a river that is perhaps five thousand miles long. Let us say that it runs from a small brook to a width of sometimes two miles, depending on where it is in it's five thousand mile journey. And its depth may be from a few inches to quite a number of feet, let us say - at some points - several hundred feet in depth.

Now, think about that in the dimensional sense so that it isn't just a flat surface and at every point then is a creative core - every point, and also at every point is a means to contact that core. Like a pellet that can be launched into that creative core and because of the truly unlimited nature of your creativity you can energize a creative point and through your conscious awareness that there is a creative core you can connect the points together by a line of energy that flows as light. Light then conveys your understanding to the point that is stimulative for you in your creative process of other creative core points that wish to join because you've invoked them into a clearer and more comprehensive creative effort.

Now, what I am doing in this material is stimulating you. I am, with light technique words, literally taking concepts and energizing them within you. We are bombarding you then with these pellets of light - light coming in conceptually now into your creative core. But now let us use in a particular exercise a means to access a creative core point mentioned earlier called the "unconditional understanding of unconditional love" and note the wording of that - unconditional understanding of unconditional love. Now keep in mind that light is interactive, it is always interacting with other levels or other creative core points beyond the one that you have recognized, so using light really is invocative of bringing together many, many, many, many creative core points and as a pebble creates a expansive environment when placed in water thus your launching a particular light probe into the creative core expands the awareness point of that probe and that's the important point here. The probing itself expands through the projectile into the creative core and through its expansive nature activates other light contact points and invokes the larger use of the creative core's vibrational flow.

Now for some of you, you may wonder about the difference between energy and light. I would say energy is a broader term. The light flow is certainly energy but energy is both a broader term and a more specific one. It is the electromagnetic or polarity aspects of manifestation.

Alright, light energy is the term used when there are many, many, vibratory or energy patterns present interacting together so creatively that a light or a means to see creatively more clearly is created so literally that circle of energy that is in our diagram is a light being or a light perspective or a magnetic effect that radiates because of its energy interactiveness that lights up a creative core. Now, light is truly unlimited and another way of looking at this example, this energy circle, is to see that this is manifested Source and you will note the word - manifested Source - this light that we are calling Source or this energy spectrum is always increasing in - and we will use the term - "wattage". The light is ever getting brighter. Why? Because the specific nature of the energy is communicating, is radiating, is invoking, is exploring, is growing, is expanding. Now when you have lit up then a creative core and it is penetrated by a projectile of light energy from another creative core you build a bridge, you keep bridging the process of one creative core to another and when they are bridged creatively enough by enough of these projectiles, whether it is in a personal sense in your creative core or in the whole sense - in its creative core - when you create so much energy that is connected that a bridge is built and the cores come together the energy becomes so invocative that they become a part of each other. There is a tremendous expansion, literally a creative explosion that allows the two creative cores to blend into one. This is why working consciously with the projectiles will allow you to merge the perspective that you have now into the potential that you are seeking. A conscious projection into that creative core done as an exercise, literally as an affirmation of the bridging process can be one of the most effective tools that we can use in triggering an unlimited understanding of any particular area.

TECHNIQUE FOR EXPANDING HEART CENTER

I would like then, to give you the specific way of using this technique. Diagram #8 shows you as an "X" that is labeled "self as I recognize it now." That "X" would include your current understanding of the love area so 8A represents the heart area. You energize, then, the heart area through your desire nature that is welcoming the progressive understanding into its clearer and clearer perspective. What I am saying here is that you want to expand the heart. There is the understanding that you've built that this is the goal. You want to expand it. And perhaps its important to see that that's a choice, that for a while, particularly on the physical plane, we do not perhaps consciously recognize that an expansion is either needed or desired in that area. You could say that you are too busy seeking to be loved to see that being loving is the prerequisite to being loved unconditionally. You must grasp that unconditional love is the goal and as I said, to grasp it you must first accept that this is the part of self that you are now attempting to energize.

Now I am not telling you that you are not loving - of course you are - whoever is reading this - you are loving. But lovingness is as unlimited as anything else and it truly is the creative core itself. It is the means to bridge all of those creative cores together through the energy interchange that this basic point represents. Now I think the Creator has done that very well. He has set up a desire within all of us to explore the love area and for a

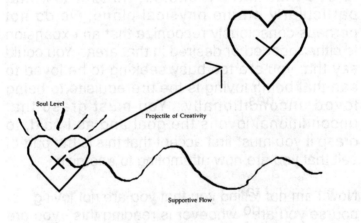

DIAGRAM #8
Self's Expansion Through The Heart

Soul Level

Projectile of Creativity

Supportive Flow

while we project it out. We project it into others to love us and it is because we are trying to understand that we are loved unconditionally by the Source itself. We are really trying to accept that and we do accept it but not yet at the unconditional level.

Now, the point of contact then that we've called the "X" is your current understanding of love and you will note the lines around the "X", the little ones that represent a radiation, a radiation has begun and the radiation comes about when you have accepted a particular point of light that is called your soul. The soul perspective literally lights up the love area enough, enough of the energy of the soul is present so that the love center begins to radiate and others begin to see that radiation and you will be told by those who can see it at this point, " I see how loving you are becoming, how the love center is growing." And you can also have eyes to see in this area and see that something has occurred. What has occurred is that the energy level that you are able to relate to on the physical plane has expanded enough so that the fine energies of the soul are penetrating to the physical level and thus invoking more light. Remember it takes a whole perspective to create light and you do not radiate very much as light on the physical plane until you bring in the soul's perspective that then lights up your energy field on the physical level. Now, some of you utilize the soul's perspective sometimes and then it seems less available at times. Does this mean the light goes away? No, it does not. It is progressive. You may not recognize that you are utilizing the

43

perspective of the flow, or the creativity of the soul. Your life may still be personality oriented. But, there is a beginning point that when you lock-in enough energy of the soul that radiation is present from that point on and I would say that if you are reading this material at all, this has occurred within you.

Probably quite a bit of understanding of the soul is present and you are quite a radiant being on the physical plane. In order to have gotten this far into this material there must be on the physical level, a response within your understanding and that response is the soul's light that now I am triggering through these word symbols that I give you. Now in the exercise the radiating "X" then is our projectile and you will note in Diagram #8 the line that is horizontal which we will call the supportive flow intersects the projectile line at the heart point within the flow.

Now, the goal is then, to view the "X", your creative projectile which is your current understanding in the heart area and allow, and this is the interesting part, allow a process that seems to create a sense of flow of the projectile into the creative core but in reality what is created, is a overlaying of the creative core into that point that we have called the projectile. In order to do that, however, one utilizes the understanding that you have already, that you are a part of something greater and thus you see the projectile in its divine flow connecting, going to, establishing contact with, energizing or any of these terms, that point in the center of the creative core that is symbolized by that small circle. The one in the center.

Now, that is the image that one uses to stimulate a point of contact that centers the creative core or allows you to energize the heart of it. What is really occurring, however, at that point is that through the point of consciousness that is radiating now, because of the soul's contact, you literally are overlaying that whole creative core into that point of consciousness. Now we are going to complete this exercise by telling you something, that if you get nothing else out of this whole exploration that I give you on all of these pages, if you get this one you've got something that is going to aid you in a very major sense.

MIRROR REVERSAL

I have stated that many of you have reversed the creative process and this is symbolized as you look in a mirror and the image is reversed. You have seen literally, the creative process as reversed. And thus, when life mirrors the creative process to you, you get a reversed image. In the same sense then, one uses your understanding of being a part of something greater to activate within self then the understanding of one's own unlimited abilities. You have accepted, anyway, most of you, and I would say, you wouldn't be reading this if you hadn't - that there is a Creator, and because of that you understand that there is a creative process that you are a part of. You have not yet understood how to,with your own efforts, create on that level also.

Certainly, one way to understand it is a major level indeed, called the Co-Creator level and I have been talking about that a lot and I will continue to talk about it. But from this point of view of reversal, it is necessary to see that a projectile which seems to be launched into a creative core that is a part of the larger process of the Whole is simply a symbol for allowing that creative process of the Whole to manifest within self. So, we will use symbols that connect you into that whole perspective because it is both a framework within which you exist and certainly it is worth recognizing that it is there and that it is supportive of your creative effort. However, it is necessary to understand or to reverse again the view that you have of how the creative process works.

I say this to you, when you have understood this point, your consciousness need not allow the mirror to reverse your image. And that is very interesting. It is not important to see on the physical level, a mirror, that doesn't reverse, but what is important is the synchronicity that says " I no longer reverse my creative process - I can see it clearly - I understand that I am able to utilize the Whole's perspective within me now." Now, for some of you, this may not seem important. Or it may not even seem to be a point at all, what I'm talking about here, but it is such a core issue that many of you have simply not any awareness of it yet at all and you will not probably on the physical plane very much. There may be a few of you that will gain this understanding of what has been reversed. To do so, one must be able to relate to creativity in a multi-dimensional manner which, let us say, creates the multi-dimensional focus that is then responsive to the overlaying system in such a comprehensive manner that all illusion about self's inability to create exactly as the Source creates fall away. That's worded very carefully my friends. Well, one begins to grasp or to be triggered in such areas by these word symbols as I bring them to you now. One gains a gradual understanding, usually, of this area. We keep, then, stimulating you creatively, or with these light triggers. Then as you open your understanding the total grasp of who you are can begin to be energized. You may notice my friends, that spiritual teachers are always very, very aware of who you really are.

We have seen the magnificence of your creative

core. Some of us more than others but generally we recognize the divine within you in a way that you are only beginning to understand.

It is then important to let go of the need to view something that seems a part of physical existence that must be accepted such as a mirroring that reverses and see that every perspective can be transcended in a ever escalating fashion as the creative core is contacted and triggers then an invocation of the unlimited nature which the creative core symbolizes. It stimulates the creative core, then stimulates the understanding of what unlimitedness really represents because unlimitedness is a symbol and I use the word a lot because it symbolizes the understanding of what creativity really is, a transcendent spiraling means to express unconditionally the Whole's inspirational flow that lovingly and allowingly surrounds and supports all that is and my friends, all that is not.

As you become aware there is a gradual letting go process. This letting go process is the enlargement of your acceptance of that creative core. The creative core is within you but you have to step back and in stepping back and allowing it to be activated the contact is broadened into the specific projectiles that will connect to this creative core in an unlimited manner. It bridges points of creativity setting up radiant light point connections that then bridge points of creativity setting up further light point connections in an unlimited expression of the unfoldment of Source itself.

Can you get a good image of that? Even if the word symbols I give you are not yet completely digested or understood, imaging or visualizing what I am giving you will contact your creative core mechanism and allow a certain amount of expansion within.

YOUR EMOTIONAL BODY IN THE DIMENSIONS

Your emotional body is a very important part of your creativity. As you seek to place what is mostly a fourth dimensional attribute in to the third dimension, however, it is necessary to understand the process and what occurs vibrationally as the structure of the third dimension energizes the emotional responses within self. I have sought to help humanity in other writings to understand that dimensions are structures or formats vibrating as vehicles within which consciousness expresses. Thus your emotional body is an aspect of consciousness. The third or fourth dimensions are the structures within which consciousness exists. Symbolically the fourth dimension equates to flow potential and your emotional body is your flow potential and thus there is a natural attraction between the vehicle which is the fourth dimension and the conscious point which is the emotional body. Thus although you may seek to function emotionally in the third dimension there is a natural attraction to the fourth dimension emotionally. This is not a "bad" effect nor is it especially "good", it simply is. But by understanding it and the nature of the third dimension then you can see more clearly and understand the goals as far as how to help your emotionally body vibrate in a manner which is an integrated use of what it is on a basic level. Or we could say, help it to be whole.

Many of you have literally fractured your emotional body. By that I mean you have beliefs that say crying, anger, loss - all of these are bad emotions.

Joy, love, fun, happiness, contentment, these are good emotions and one should express the good emotions and let go of the bad ones. Now I am not advocating in this material emotions such as fear, loss, anger, anxiety, frustration but I am saying that we should create in a symbol an emotional body that is a circle and say that in a vibrational sense every emotion, whether it is considered "good" or "bad", has a particular frequency or vibratory point in that circle. The goal of course, remember, is to use your whole emotional body so that you don't leave out or let go of those "bad" emotions without including the vibrational points that those particular emotions vibrate to in a manner that wipes out or releases the fractured effect. It is necessary to see that you can never destroy a part of yourself. You simply incorporate that part in a way that gives it a guidance level that is beyond its comprehension and thus the use of that point serves a purpose, let us say, that is clearer.

A good example of this is the ego which is the center of the personality. Now you may have been taught that you get rid of the ego. You get rid of it. Well, in my opinion that isn't very logical. You have carefully, lifetime over lifetime built up this strong ego centered personality and it has a use, a function. Certainly you want to let go of the perspective that this ego at the center of your personality is your guiding system as you function in your creative effort within physical existence but this perspective is a strength and you don't throw it out. You place it within a larger perspective which is called the soul. And you allow its strength to be guided by that larger perspective which the soul represents.

51

Going back now to that part of your emotional body that vibrates as loss, fear, anxiety - you may have given that a lot of energy in the past. It has a strong energy sense then. It knows how to function "well". Now you don't want to allow the part of the emotional body that has been strongly energized to guide your life if it is not an emotion that is serving you well but you can't throw it out. It simply will not go if you will. And you will keep reactivating it or the use of emotions which are not serving you well until you do the following with it; you include it in the process! Now, again I want to emphasize that I don't mean the emotion itself but the energy point that vibrates with that particular emotion must be included in a energy wholeness that is your emotional body. This fractured point which says "I give up who I am. I let go of who I am in order to become something greater - a part of me is destroyed," must be clearly seen as counterproductive to your evolutionary process. You could say you give to your evolutionary process the vibrations of what you have been as the fuel for becoming something greater - you don't throw it away.

You put it in the process - in the pot if you will - and stir it up with all of the current desires to be something greater. The desire nature or your emotional responses then are literally in the creative sense the fuel which flows you to your creative goal. Now think about it, if you have been one that used the emotional body extensively, you have a lot of energy invested in it.

Now, let us say that you are not that, at least you don't think you are, you are one that has a very mental perspective and at this point you don't validate your emotional body very much. Well, I guarantee you this - you have in the past or you wouldn't be at this point in your evolution. You have, all of you, invested a lot of energy in the emotional body because it is such a vital component of who and what you are that you can't flow into a larger state of being without having expressed this emotional point of view comprehensively. Thus if you find you are currently burying emotions or seeking to destroy them, which is probably the same thing for most of you, then I give you the following light techniques and methods to aid you to see how to use that energy point, whatever it may be, as an impetus into your evolution.

Light probing techniques create an attraction that brings to you an integrated point of view which encompasses more of the creative flow or energy. Now, this Diagram #9 shows you a circle that represents your emotional body and I have placed around that circle certain emotions. Now, I have not listed every emotion because to do so would take more room than is necessary. It is not then, a complete list of emotions. But I've tried in a graduated sense to give you a sense of which emotions have a lot of energy in them and which do not as far as a physical level vibration is concerned. Now you will note that unconditional love doesn't seem to have a lot of energy in it on the physical plane and in my opinion that's because it hasn't been used very much on the

DIAGRAM #9

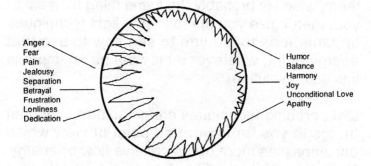

Anger
Fear
Pain
Jealousy
Separation
Betrayal
Frustration
Lonliness
Dedication

Humor
Balance
Harmony
Joy
Unconditional Love
Apathy

physical plane. Also, the joy level and some of the other very "positive" emotions have comparatively little energy invested in them on the physical plane. Some of the emotions may surprise you, either in the amount of energy that is in them or the lack of energy that is in them. Now I've tried to show you from the vibratory flow of the circle the amount of energy in each emotions. It is a generalization but I have placed the emotions in the progressive order of the amount of energy that they use on the physical plane. We could then, show the flow which is your emotional body as a river, the wide vibratory rate is the physical level of the river and at a particular point that river becomes very fine vibrationally and you will note that the "higher" emotions fit into that particular energy spectrum that is a finer vibrational flow.

Going back again to the emotional body as a circle, look at what would occur if you tried to throw away or get rid of all of the vibration that you consider to be "bad". You really cut off a great deal more than half of the emotional body as it can function physically within you now. The goal of course is to dimensionalize the emotional body and I'm going to explain that in a moment, so that all points in the circle can be energized without the "heavy" effect that keeps you caught into this third dimensional point without the ability to access again the fourth dimensional flow.

The third dimension represents the enlargement or magnification of the creative process literally taking your creativity and putting it under a microscope so that you can take it apart, see what makes it tick if you will, and put it back together easily and clearly. But in the process of taking it all apart emotionally the emotional body gets kind of fractured. Part of it pulled into the third dimension but because of its natural attraction to the fourth dimension a split can occur. Now your physical body has been focused on the third dimension up until this point for almost all of you. Your mental body is more easily able to penetrate beyond the third dimension into the fourth, fifth, and perhaps a reflection of the sixth depending upon your point of evolution but for many of you that are reading this material your mental body has functioned very well within the fifth dimension which is divine structure.

Now, you see there is a certain compatibility between the fifth and the third dimension that doesn't exist between the third and the fourth dimension and I am not saying that they are incompatible but I am saying that many of you have seen the third dimension and the fifth dimension seems a natural extension of it. But you haven't been able to access the fourth dimension in connection with the third. Now I am generalizing here. This is one perspective that is quite often buried and it may be that some of you will not recognize what I am telling you. Know that I am not talking about your conscious awareness as much as your creative point of view - that ability to create your life which is very much a part of the subconscious process. Your awareness then vibrationally of what the dimensions represent is that for a while physical existence seems to be a very confining structure and it is easier to understand a structural dimension such as the fifth dimension than a flow dimension such as the fourth dimension. So the mental body is generally quite comfortable both on the third dimension and in the fifth dimension, but the emotional body yearns for the fourth dimension and doesn't like the third dimension and certainly doesn't understand the fifth dimension.

Now, the key for it is understanding the fifth in order to understand the third and that is very important. The reason is this; if we equate the fourth dimension to a flow then we could equate the fifth dimension to the supportive nature that facilitates the flow. I have many times used the example of the river bed being the supportive nature that guides the flow of the river in the directional sense that will allow it to express clearly. In other words, if a rivers banks are not there, it scatters its energy or its flow, doesn't it? It floods over into an area where it is dissipated and less effective. Thus going back to our example - the fourth dimensional flow which we could equate then as the emotional flow functioning as a mechanism for the divine plan is stretched in its understanding by uniting with the fifth dimensional expression which could be equated then to the supportive mechanism of the divine flow.

Now you are seeking balance from every point of view and thus your emotional body and its structure can learn from your mental body and its structure. They are the natural balancing tools of each other. The mental body in its understanding of concepts can be used to help the emotional body see beyond a more limited perspective that is a flowing one but perhaps not as aware of the whole picture as the mental responses are. On the other hand, the mental body has a tendency sometimes to analyze too much and the emotional body can flow the mental body out of that energy point that is being reiterated in an out-of-balance sense. Thus, they are good partners if then, on the physical plane, we are trying to show the emotional perspective how to be a whole one, we begin by allowing the emotional body to enter a perspective that is fifth dimensional. I have a particular exercise to begin this process.

ACCEPTING OR INTEGRATING THE FULL ENERGY OF THE EMOTIONAL BODY

1.   Visualize a crystal city. There are buildings of various heights made out of crystal and there are streets and roadways between them. There are nice long streets and roadways - a nice flow of streets and roadways. Now visualize your emotional body as a river and allow it to flow into the crystal city. Let's visualize it as gold and the crystal city is of course clear. Bring the river in and see how it fills up the streets and roadways of your crystal city. Now what occurs? There's great beauty there isn't there? The clear crystal reflects the gold and the gold reflects the clear crystal. There is a good compatibility as the two join together. Now, spend enough time so you sense a good joining, a good coming together of the crystal structure and the golden flow knowing that one represents the emotional and one the mental. Now when you sense a complete joining of it then go on to number Two.

2.   Utilize a new symbol knowing that it incorporates the crystal city from both the flow and the crystal structure point of view and let us use the symbol of blue energy. Now, lets equate it to a blue circle and it is alive with electrical energy. It leaps high. Creatively electrical surges and connections are being made within the blue energy. As you view the circle then, do the following which is point Three.

3.   You have a magnifying glass and look within it now at the blue circle so that you can enlarge

and see the circle magnified ten times. Look at it and what do you notice? Well as the power multiplies you will notice and see more clearly the electrical nature of the energy. You will see there are spaces between the electrical connections but you will see the electrical surges and flow quite clearly.

4.　　I ask you to again get another magnifying glass and multiply again what has already been multiplied once and you will note that in the second expansion there are very large, large spaces where no activity takes place. It is into these points that I wish you to recycle, if you will, the energy which you are seeking to release or as you have termed it "get rid of" in the areas of loss, anxiety, pain, frustration, anger - whatever emotion is not serving you well. Each of these emotions has a vibratory correspondence and I'd like you to do the following:

5.　　Seek to feel a particular emotion, in other words - get into that emotion, yes, anger or loss or whatever it is, get into that emotion. As you wear, then, that emotion it is active enough for you now to take that specific vibration and place it in the spaces within this greatly enlarged perspective of the blue energy. As you do that, if you are embodying that emotion when you do it you will notice an electrical surge that helps to fill up that space that is a part of your potential creativity that you haven't yet activated. Thus you've included the energy that hasn't been serving you well into a creative effort to integrate the emotional body. You've released the need to express the "bad"

You've released the need to express the "bad" emotion but allowed its energy to be included in the blue energy which, remember, represents a creative joining of the emotional and mental body areas. You use also the fourth and fifth dimensions which will now be explored third dimensionally by means of this magnification process so you really integrate the third, the fourth and the fifth dimensions and the emotional and mental perspective by means of energy that you thought you just had to get rid of or throw away.

As you become more conscious you can purposefully utilize what seems to be waste products in a manner that is consciously invocative of your own evolution and integration of all of the bodies expressing in a balanced manner now.

Now you might just say to me well if I throw away the bad emotions doesn't the Whole just recycle that energy and use it? And my answer is "yes, of course, but the goal is for you to be consciously aware of your creativity as being able to utilize every energy opportunity that you choose to utilize. You don't have to utilize every opportunity - I'm not saying that but I'm saying when you choose to utilize an energy opportunity you can." There is then a conscious awareness that you have at the tips of your creative fingertips all of the energy tools that are necessary to expand your awareness through this workshop that has been called physical existence. You need not ever say to self "my, what can I do now?" Because if you look around you will know that the tools that you need are there for you and you can always keep expanding your

Let us say then that you place as much of the "bad" emotion as you can within this creative space that symbolizes to your subconscious mind a space within which to keep connecting that particular emotion. It is not a one time event at all. It shows the creative effort of yourself where a particular creative dumping ground can be and part of the emotional frustration that you sometimes get into is "what do I do now with what is not serving me well?" You see you may try to shake it off but have you ever tried to shake off something that was magnetically attached to you? It's very difficult because it keeps coming back. You keep attracting it back again. You can shake, and shake and its magnetically pulled to you again. When you cut that magnetic connection in this way you create a magnetic attraction in a more productive way and that allows your creativity to fill up in a manner which will make specific connections and keep the means to expand it further.

You really build a corridor that is important and a permanent means to keep yourself supplied with the means to enlarge the core integration that you have begun to express. You may have a question of "is it necessary to release the energy tied up in each of these emotions and restructure it into the blue energy?" I would say yes. The emotions need to be creatively recycled in this manner or included in the creative process and I would include the ones that you consider to be "good" because you sometimes release those also. You may not wish to, at this point, but if you close off the love center sometimes in an erroneous belief that it is necessary, then what happens to that energy? Well how about placing a corridor of energy also for it back into itself you might say or into the point of creativity that the magnification of the blue energy represents as we discussed it before. I would then, spend the time to embody or bring into your conscious awareness each one of these particular emotions. First of all - embody them so you can feel them - until they vibrate within you and then place that vibratory feeling within the spaces of the magnified blue electrical energy. Now it will work as well for you as you connect into it so its probably important not to do all of the emotions at once, to really wait until you get "the hang of it". One must feel it entering that field of blue energy, sense the vibratory connection being made and then it wouldn't hurt to envision a flow of energy that is permanently being made from that particular point on the circle into the blue field that you are creatively envisioning. You could say it is a penetration through the emotional body into the creative core of self as it is magnified through the emotional and mental bodies functioning on the fourth and fifth dimension and then magnified into the third dimension.

As we continue our discussion of the emotional body, it becomes clear that emotions are only difficult when they are not able to access a flow. Now that may seem a difficult subject because isn't a loss a flow? No, it isn't. It is a stuck perspective that keeps reiterating loss. Just as frustration is a stuck perspective that keeps reiterating there is a sense of being stuck in connection with those emotions that are not considered productive. In the higher emotions or those that vibrate less the higher emotions or those that vibrate less concretely, there is less reality in connection with them so there is a whole different means of identifying these higher emotions and therein comes one of the seeming paradoxical statements about emotion that has not yet been fully explored and understood by those of you on the physical plane. Higher emotions are accessing points that allow a flow. They never simply go around in a circle or remain a stuck perspective. They contact a creative core which is expansive. They vibrate in harmony with the pulse, the beat, the rhythm, of the plan. There is a compatibility that when one is vibrating with those emotions says "I am a part of all that is - I am all that is - I am aware that all that is vibrates here within me." The emotions that are considered "bad" have, on the third dimension, been magnified but keep signaling limitation by leaping over or not validating these connective points that the "good" vibrations represent so that the stuckness factor connected or energized through the "bad" emotions simply are a point that cannot access the alignment process while in this vibratory state.

I give you yet another example and in Diagram #10 you will note that each emotion has its own rate. I give it to you as a specific line. Now on those emotions that are considered "bad" there is a line where they end and you will note a wavy line that really represents the creative flow as you are seeking it. Now there is a barrier or a gapped effect then between that particular emotion and the creative flow. Now sometimes the emotion will leap the gap and enter the creative flow. That

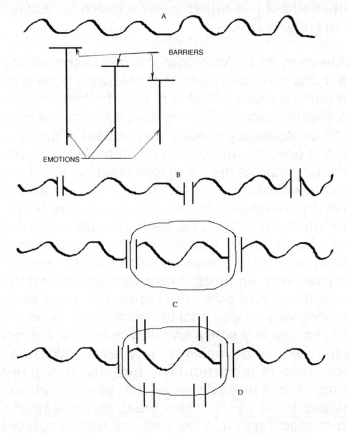

DIAGRAM #10

A

BARRIERS

EMOTIONS

B

C

D

of compatibility as far as that basic flow is concerned. It might also be a vibration that is close vibrationally to the love, joy, happiness and so forth in the circle. Then that is an emotion that is easily released and placed in your creative core. There's usually no difficulty in doing so at the basic level anyway, you may occasionally have this emotion but it is rather easily allowed to become that creative flow.

However, let us look now at some of the energy that has a vibratory rate that creates a large gap. In the first place it is very difficult for that emotion to leap the gap and join the flow, if it does however, and occasionally it does, it creates, I'm going to use the word - havoc in your life. Many of the mental hospitals are full of those that have had this occur without the means to integrate then the heavily energized emotion into the creative flow in a manner that could be used productively. You may have known or seen someone who paced back and forth spouting words that made no sense, very agitated, there was a tremendous amount of energy or flow present. They were moving very much - a lot of energy - but the words don't make any sense and they are not in contact with a sense of reality on any level. What has occurred is a particularly heavily energized emotion has leaped beyond that barrier that was placed there by your own creativity to keep you from reacting in this isolated and non-integrated manner. If the emotion does erroneously leap the barrier then you have energized this creative flow and accessed it by this emotion. You've perhaps, we could say, stuck a electrical probe into the flow we could say, stuck a electrical probe into the flow but as it flows back at you through that probe you get burned by it - you begin to burn out creative circuitry thus creating gaps within that flow and you will see Diagram #10B showing those points that intersect the gaps and then the next Diagram #10C will show you the loops of energy, of creative energy, that one gets stuck in between those creative gaps.

Now one loops from one gap to the other because the flow is not integrated. There isn't any way to access it in a manner that uses any sort of a support system. There is no structural sense present within this accessing, the emotion is simply completely out of control and has leaped into a creative flow and short circuited that creative flow. This can be very damaging, both to the emotional and physical structures, and has been treated by your doctors through shock treatments. What occurs is a shutting down of the loop of activity through the shocks to the brain area. You will notice in the next Diagram #10D that the loop now has gaps in it itself and thus the pattern of frenzied activity that keeps looping has now been broken through the shock treatments. After the breaking up of this energy loop, whether it is through the shock treatments or not, and I'm not advocating shock treatments, I'm not. But in one sense or another something is needed to stop that looping effect. There are several things that can stop it. One, an intervention on the human level through shock treatments; Two, the death process that allows you to access a new physical structure and a new beginning creatively on the physical plane;

Three, the penetration of the soul which attracts an energy mass or plug from the spiritual plane and is literally invoked through what one might call spiritual intervention. This has been termed divine grace. To me that means that many times a stuck perspective on the physical plane can only be mitigated or transformed by a spiritual perspective entering and pulling that stuck physical perspective out of its point of muddle that its gotten itself into. Thus, in some way, the looping must be released and again an effort to understand the use of the emotional body beyond the shattering or scattered effect that takes that whole circle of energy and uses it only in one area which energizes it so much that it bursts inappropriately from the natural guidelines that have been placed there to protect the creative flow.

What that means then is the Creator has literally set up some guidelines for learning and as long as you know what they are and work within them it's rather easy to learn and grow. You only get yourself into predicaments or stuck when you go against the flow as its been set up for you. Now I'm not saying that you consciously choose to use the emotional body in a manner that is unproductive but in one sense you do because you perhaps choose not to validate the natural balancer of the emotional body which is the mental body. If you persistently ignore the balancing tools available then you get yourself into predicaments or stuck points that create a need to take it all back to the drawing board and begin again in a creative sense.

These important points where one feels very, very, very, very stuck are usually where you have in one body or another reached a point where a particular non-productive perspective has been so heavily energized that it has leaped natural boundaries and is trespassing in your creative flow in a way that can no longer flow. It gets into a loop and spins around in that loop until it is pulled out by the clearer perspective on the spiritual plane and must begin again to sort out the process and see more clearly certain available choices that have been made available to it but have been ignored. There has been a conscious, and I repeat, a conscious choice to not take advantage of the opportunities that have been given to it. One does not always say "I want to stay here stuck in this perspective," I'm not saying that - many of you have not worked a great deal to release the perspective that your emotional body currently occupies but you have not yet seen that there are many tools available and that, perhaps, your divine responsibility is to seek to use them. If one method doesn't work for you find another and another until you do find what works for you in transcending the perspective of the emotional body that shatters its integrated flow. The integrated flow will access that creative flow of the Whole; of all of your creativity without burning out its contact point in a way that creates these gapped effects in the creative flow. Can you see then that the integration of the emotional body which is your accessing tool to the creative flow is an extremely important point and key for you now.

RELEASING THE DESTRUCTIVE FOCUS

We will continue with many more techniques in this part of our journey but it is the basic ability to see that you must choose now to use these tools or some tools that will allow the change that you wish. There is sometimes a belief that to be balanced you need to remain in an emotional isolated state. The excitement of existence is what is attractive to you - you are excited by it and this is the emphasis that you wish on the physical plane. Now I am not telling you that life can not be exciting - it can - in a creative sense. What I am saying is that there are stuck points such as you see in your modern day newspapers. The sensationalism then that is expressed - the crashes of airplanes, the deaths, the murders, the massacres, the shootings - all of these things, these sensational acts are points of excitability that for an instant allow the emotional body to sense a creative point and it is seeking to sense a creative point. However, that habit pattern that is formed to sense that creative point of sensation through a destructive focus is something that needs to be released rather than expressed.

Can you see that this is part of what we talked about earlier. There is a habit of energizing the points that are not serving you well. Here before we were talking about an emotion that wasn't serving you well; now we are talking about an act on the physical plane that isn't serving you well - a plane crash, a murder, sensationalism of all kinds is being energized and then it erroneously seeks to leap into that creative flow and you believe that is the only accessing tool that you have into the creative flow. I would say this is an important point in the mass consciousness of humanity and keeps being emphasized over and over again and it certainly is a looped effect - can you see that? That as the planet, the earth, seeks to create a new age it is focusing on those non-productive, excitable points that I'm calling sensationalism that flow on emotion that isn't serving you well and if they are heavily enough energized and they have been on this planet, then they leap into the creative flow. They create then, because of the very nature of them, an interruption or a gap - an interruptive point of the creative flow and then the earth's creativity loops around and can't get out of that loop that the sensationalism is always energizing.

What needs to occur to release that loop that is distressed and distorted is the specific energy of an event such as the Harmonic Convergence that makes available a light energy and remember - the light is a connective factor that then smoothes out this loop and although the loop may still be there, it has less disruption within it. Eventually the looping will be gone through the acceptance of this light energy but it is necessary to see that the sensationalism is an irritant that must be consciously released also. The mass consciousness must be willing to give up this excitability factor that activated these loops and disruptive portions of the creative flow on your earth. The productive connections of your mass media can be helpful as soon as this sensationalism is released. Now I know that the answer - the response from the newspapers will be "that's what sells newspapers" but its a loop. Until the earth is willing at one point or another to break that loop it will continue. The key, it seems to me, are those that have the spiritual sight to see such a loop. By energizing of a clear point of view and making it available to the public they will then begin to energize a whole different way of relating and creating on the earth.

HELPING THE EMOTIONAL BODY TO USE THE THIRD DIMENSION

Your emotional body learns very rapidly, that is true, it may not be able to hold the perspective that it has learned but it learns rapidly. We can utilize then this strength in the learning area and let us do so through the following exercise:

See a green circle which represents the emotional body. It is there before you - you are visualizing it - now it is large enough that you can take your physical body into it so I ask you to visualize this large green circle and then literally step into it. Now it is also thick enough that you can get inside of it and you know that you are then surrounded on the physical plane by this green focus that represents your emotional body at its ideal level and in its wholeness. It is a complete reference to the emotional body as you then stand within this green circle. All of its potential comes into you, all points within this circle are inputting to you - you have allowed the whole perspective of your emotional potential to come into you.

Now as you stand within this green circle sense in the heart chakra an opening. Literally the energy that is coming in from the green circle is certainly surrounding the physical body. It is also pouring into the heart area on the etheric (chakra) level as well as the physical level. Literally you can allow now an unlimited amount of energy to come into the heart area and as you visualize the whole emotional response coming into the heart area you will either sense it physically or know that the heart

71

is expanding. There will be a sense of activity in that area and that activity is the use of the emotions that come through the physical perspective and then are energized as a whole perspective and then placed within the heart and therein lies the important point here: you will remember the material that I've just given in that the emotional body has an affinity for the fourth dimension that it is not very well integrated within the third dimension. By seeing it as a whole symbolically within the third dimension and then standing within that green circle which represents your whole emotional potentiality within the third dimension you bring together for the emotional body the understanding that it can "get its act together" in the third dimension and as I said, it learns very rapidly thus as it unites its perspective within the third dimension it can pour that integrated response into the heart area. Now, integration and the heart are very compatible and because the energy is integrated the heart responds very readily to it, is very sensitive to such an integrated response, opens easily and well and then begins to send out a radiating effect within the third dimensional spectrum and that is important because it begins to build within the third dimension an integrated vehicle through your heart area and that can be an important key that has been missing for many of you. You could call it the missing link - that you skip to the fourth dimension before being able to access very much of the emotional wholeness or integrated response that you are seeking. You've left out integration within the third dimension and remember - you really can't throw anything away, you can't skip over anything, leave anything out or throw anything away - the goal is - integration of everything into the creative core - everything must be included and if you have not included something then you, perhaps at one point or another, are allowed to go back and pick it up again and thus include it.

There is no way to leave anything out. It must be included so perhaps the most important thing that you are seeking to understand emotionally is that you can have an integrated response emotionally within the third dimension. Now, some of you then take the emotional body to the fourth dimension and it works quite well there for you. It may not be completely integrated - in point of fact - it is not but there is more ability to utilize a larger or more integrated part of it than within the third dimension.

Now, those of you that consider yourselves to be quite emotional, you have emotional responses that come forth easily, you do have your emotional body mostly focused on the fourth dimension. Those of you that consider yourself to be mental in responses and have buried your emotions; you see you have the mental body then focused on the fifth dimension and the fifth sees structure and thus it is really literally, in the fullest sense, trying to balance your whole life including the emotional body. But the emotional body in order to be balanced needs to also utilize the third dimension as well as the fourth and literally what occurs if you are burying your emotions is the emotions are caught literally between the third and the fourth or between the fourth and the fifth, you could say they fall through the cracks - they get buried there and you don't validate them. You can't enlarge or view them in the third dimension because they are not truly functioning there and you can't get into the flow of them in the fourth dimensional sense because they aren't there either - they have fallen through the cracks between the third and the fourth or between the fourth and the fifth dimensions.

Now, certain analyses that we may give to you may show them functioning in a particular dimension, we really have not developed an analysis tool that shows emotions falling through the cracks but in the buried sense this is true and many times we can see the effect by knowing that they don't flow at all - they are simply buried and what they're buried in is the non-use of a structure within which to function. You aren't using them and therefore they aren't in a particular structure at all. Now, this is perhaps simplifying in a sense, meaning that there are some of you that again have this fractured response, part of the emotions are buried dimensionally and part are not so there may be a "mixed bag" effect or this further splitting of the emotional body. Remember then, that the dimensions are the vehicle within which the consciousness functions and if you use them to bury a response then you no longer have them as a carrier of the emotions or whatever other point of consciousness we are discussing.

Our subject is the emotional body but keep in mind that in the sense of looking at the dimensions and how one responds to them we could give you information on all of the bodies and how they function dimensionally, in point of fact, I intend to just that - helping you to relate to the four body system which is the spectrum of your consciousness and its vibrational flow as we look at it specifically in regard to certain sections of it. Again, you could equate your consciousness to a whole divided into four pieces and you would have your spiritual, mental, emotional and physical perspective and even if you are not functioning physically at the moment, which of course you are, but even when you are not - there is within that whole perspective a part of you which either has been or will be physical because on the spiritual level you are not in sequential time so there is always a physical perspective, at least in the way that the Source has divided up energy on this cosmic day experience. We do need to see that the framework is different for each cosmic day experience - but in the one that we are currently experiencing and for, let us say, quite a number preceding days there has been a physical point of view.

It is important as you stand within this green circle and accept into your heart chakra the energy of this whole circle that you feel your physical body, that you know literally you are standing in the third dimension. You don't want to get it into the fourth dimension entirely. Now, of course, in relating to the chakra level it enters the fourth dimension and that's alright, that's fine but allow it to be a multidimensional experience. You are including also, because of the structure of the chakra system, the fifth dimension but what you are all learning to do, although we haven't discussed it yet is to be multidimensional, to use, let us say, the integrated way of relating dimensionally using strengths of each dimension together in an integrated focus which of course is what the Source is able to do but for a while we take the process apart - we look at it specifically in each area to see what needs to be more clearly understood and we then awaken to the fact that all of this is simultaneous, that there is no sequential point of view at all, except for the learning of the "how to make it work clearly" process and I say that is quite important.

All of you understand that spiritually there is only the eternal now and that is an absolute point of view that you will recognize more and more as you gain a clearer understanding of how the divine process works. However, the Source has developed a method which we call physical existence which is sequential so that you may progress your understanding of how to utilize the process. That does not mean that after physical existence there isn't still a learning format but it is not the same, it is not sequential because by the time you have gained an understanding of the process, let us say of the structure, of the dimensional structure and how to use it simultaneously or in an integrated sense that dimensional structure becomes supportive then of your conscious expansion. The expansion then takes place not by unfolding particular aspects one step at a time but in an integrated sense so that you step to a rhythm or a beat that is illuminating but is not sequential.

Now, to really understand that, one must begin to glimpse the process of what integration truly means and how to be an integrated being. The Physical plane and the four body system allows your spiritual perspectives, as you recognize them on the physical plane, and your mental perspectives, emotional perspective, and physical perspective to create your life in a balanced manner. This is the key to understanding the integrative manner of creating which opens up the whole spectrum of understanding concerning development that is spiraling but is not sequential. There is a need then to glimpse what integration truly means before you can grasp non-sequential evolution.

Going back now to our example of allowing the emotional body in its third dimensional integrated state to input energy to your heart as you continue to allow it, and I would say it is important to sit in this space in that green circle and allow it for about 15 minutes. Now, you may activate some old patterning by doing this, perhaps there are still some beliefs that say it is difficult to open your heart, or "it doesn't work out." Perhaps there isn't a reality level yet as to what that really means. For some of you there is a sense of betrayal that may manifest from so opening or a fear of the unknown. Thus trust must join our visualization as a tool to allow the positive response from the heart after the energy is input to it through your emotional body's integrated state within the third dimension.

SLIDING AFFIRMATIONS INTO THE LAKE

Now, there are many ways of allowing yourself to activate a more ideal way of life but I wish to give you one now that is being used extensively within the Foundation and is extremely helpful. It is termed the "Lake". What you do is this: You view your subconscious mind as a lake and you see it as a specific color. Now, just ask your knowingness what color that is and it really doesn't matter what color but get a specific one or perhaps a combination of one or two, some people get blue-green for example. Now, this lake as I've stated, represents your subconscious mind and you have a slide that comes into the lake. Now we are going to give you some affirmations to slide into the lake and the goal is to return the lake to a clear color that is iridescent, sparking. It has within that iridescent effect truly every color of the rainbow, but it is crystal clear. The affirmations then, will make this lake change color. Now we truly, in the fullest sense, are not adding anything to the lake, what we are doing is activating the ideal which is already within it but perhaps you haven't recognized or realized enough to utilize it clearly. The slide then allows the ideal to be energized and as much of that ideal as you are ready for can be then consciously allowed to access the subconscious and thus a bridge is built to that ideal. Certainly it takes more than one time to reach the ideal state meaning that the more you work with these affirmations, the more you slide them in, the sooner you will be able to hold onto the ideal perspective. If it is an area that is very important for you, you may wish to do this exercise daily for a while and perhaps after about two weeks of doing it daily to assess the effect that is then created, you may need to continue or perhaps to reframe the affirmations a little after that time into an adjacent area.

Now, because you do bring up some resistance to affirmations, in other words as you slide in the affirmations your subconscious may contain certain beliefs that say whatever I'm affirming is not possible because in the past it didn't work out that way you need to recognize that working with affirmations does activate the subconscious so that you may gain a clearer perspective in a particular area it is necessary to be aware of that and to allow then a particular technique that will help you to deal with such resistance.

The first part of the technique is this: within the center of your lake is an electric light bulb and its wattage is as great as you need it, you can literally turn up the wattage. Now it has then electric-magnetic energy and if an affirmation has difficulty sliding in to the lake because of resistance then you can turn up the wattage in this electric bulb and it will slide in and be attracted to that centered point within your lake or subconscious mind. The Soul, the light of the Soul can be used for filling in the "cracks" that yet remain as you attempt to bridge any points that exist between what you consciously want in your conscious mind - what you desire consciously - and what you have stored in the subconscious creative vehicle called the subconscious mind. The Soul has then, as we have talked before, a light and radiant point of view that can be very helpful in an integrative process.

After completing your session, in which you put in affirmations, see surrounding the lake a radiance coming in to it all around - a golden radiance - it surrounds the lake and it comes into the center where your lightbulb is. I would create consciously a contact with that lightbulb - in other words emphasize it - it comes literally to the surface but you know there is that electrical magnetic core that goes from the foundation of your lake to the surface. Its really a core of energy now that you are envisioning instead of the physically shaped lightbulb that you are familiar with. Now, the golden energy moves through the lake, it is attracted to the light in the center but it comes in literally surrounding the lake and it moves gradually through the crystal clear lake water. Now as it moves through it the lake itself takes on this golden hue. What has been crystal clear then becomes, let us call it, penetrated by the gold radiation until the whole lake then is this gold radiating point that has within its center the ability to pull in from the whole an integrated point of view that we are calling the gold energy. So literally the lake accepts integration and you see it coming in from around the lake until in its electrical magnetic invocation the light in the center accepts the golden energy completely and what you will sense is the gold being accepted on every level - the surface and down into the lake clear to the bed or foundation of the lake and that is important. It doesn't have to take long, just sit there until you know that the whole lake is golden and that the electrical core has accepted this integrated golden state on all levels.

RELEASING HABIT PATTERNS OF THE EMOTIONAL BODY IN DEALING WITH TRAUMA

Your emotional body, more than any other of the four bodies, becomes what I might call "stuck" in habit patterns. And as you seek to create a network of light within self the emotional body is often the key to freeing up stuck points. Light flows, it is a means to transcend, to explore. However, if the emotional body holds on or resists the flow, the change, the exploration, there is a less than cohesive exploration made. Now, your emotional body and its input to the subconscious mind is extremely important. At the Source level it was the desire nature of the Source itself that created all that is, thus the desire nature inputs to the creative mechanism of self. The most important thing to recognize about your emotions is that they are, you might say, the manifestation of what you realize within your heart center and this is important - now, in a structural sense then your emotional body is that energy, that life force, that basically flows from the generative point or the heart center. We could call it the beginning of manifestation on any level. The heart, the generative center creates everything but by its very nature the emotional body is created first.

Now, this may sound like a contradiction to material given before or to your understanding of how creation takes place. Do we not need the mental responses to direct the creative process? This is true in the fullest sense but the emotion, the desire nature sparks that point where creation begins. That point, or that possibility is literally the emotional body. It is not yet cognizant, at that point, of all that is possible for it to be, or for it to create. It needs the mental point of view in order to balance out its complete understanding. Now we are talking at a very basic level and the emotional body at that level is not the same as you experience the emotional body on the physical plane. But my point is that the desire nature is the generative point through its flow from the heart center. It is then the expression of the heart center in a way that the other bodies do not represent. Certainly the heart is the generative point for all manifestation, but the emotional or the desire nature contacts the possibilities. Alright, thus this next Diagram #11 shows you a circle with a dot in the center. That dot represents the desire to manifest the desire nature in a basic sense, not as you know it on the physical plane, but you can use this basic contact point on the physical plane to break up points of crystallization within the emotional body.

Going back now to my opening remarks in this section, I stated that the emotional body can get stuck or caught, in a particular habit pattern of behavior along with this you need to be aware that when you use particular clearing methods to aid the emotional body and it can get caught or stuck also within these particular methods. Therefore if you have been working with removing patterns using the system advocated extensively through the foundation you might consider now another system. The reason is this: pattern removal after a certain point can become "habitual" and it no longer is as effective. I wish to explain this rather

DIAGRAM #11

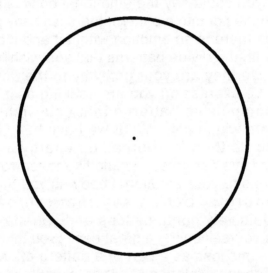

comprehensively. The reason for taking out patterns is to break up energy within the subconscious, energy that is caught and stuck into a blocked perspective and is not flowing in the manner that you wish. This energy is of course your creativity - that is what the subconscious is - truly, a vehicle for your creativity. Thus if the block is there we have taught you to break up the energy through a visual technique.

Now, you could say the emotional body is always the connector into a pattern, there isn't any pattern unless there is an emotion within it and that is as true with the divine patterns that you wish to keep because they are your gateway to the unlimited creative expression you are seeking as it is with the compulsive patterns that you wish not to validate within self. What we have been asking you to do then is to break up energy in these compulsive patterns. I would like to tell you what happens to your emotional body as you do break up energy. Let us say that the pattern compulsively contains loss and you may have found yourself crying a great deal. You then begin to see this loss as a part of a pattern of behavior and through exploring it, either by yourself or with the help of others on whatever level, you recognize or are told about a pattern and then you take it out of the subconscious through a technique, a visual technique that shows the subconscious what to remove.

Now there is never a need to worry about a pattern leaving a hole in the subconscious. That does not occur but what does occur within your emotional body is this. First, it takes the pressure out of the emotional body - it depressurizes it. This loss pattern has built up so much that it has surfaced.

If you have removed let us say, thousands of patterns, and some of you have, you get to the point where the subconscious mind cannot deal with loss or forms a habit of dealing with loss through pattern removal. The emotional body then may form a habit of handling emotions in a particular way, and I am only using the pattern removal as an example. Let us look at another way you may have handled loss. Perhaps the way you've handled loss over and over is to bury it within you. Some handle it by running home to their parents. Whatever way you handle an emotion over and over and over again in the same manner a habit pattern can build up and your emotional body becomes dependent upon it.

Then I would suggest the following: that you vary from time to time the way that you work with your emotional body to balance it. Certainly within the Foundation this is the main reason why we change our methods of clearing occasionally. It's to balance any habit patterns that may be establishing themselves within the emotional body. I would like now to give you a technique that will help you because although you may progress to another method of clearing there may be times when you wish to use an older method, such as the pattern removal and it is appropriate in some situations. However, the habit can be a definite deterrent to doing this unless we now develop, which I propose to do, certain light techniques that will break down the habit dependent nature of the emotional body.

We will call the habit pattern of the emotional body a crystallized state or a stuck perspective. Even though emotion is a flow you could look at the crystallization as a part of the flow that resists the flow or creates a energy involvement that is "sharp" with a quality that does not allow you to express the full intent that your generative center within the heart is seeking to express. Let us then establish a light technique that deals with such habit patterns, establish a means of visualizing the emotional body releasing these crystallized points through a light interaction. I think you will find it helpful to use this technique no matter what sort of processing you are using emotionally and even if you are not using any particular techniques for your emotional body at this point. Your life is processing your emotional body and thus crystallized patterns that are habitual have been formed.

Look at the following Diagram #11 , a circle with a point in the center. Now, as you look at that point in the center it grows until it is a sun and it shines - there is a light that radiates from the core of that sun. See that core radiating forth. Now, the generative point - remember - is the emotion, the desire nature of Source itself. Now it comes through the heart center, the heart establishes that desire contact and the manifested state through the desire nature is the sun. It is electrical in nature, radiant in quality and as you watch it the rays stream out until they touch every point of the circle. Look at that circle then as filling up with the rays of the sun. We will, to simplify our approach here, simply equate that sun and its rays that fill the circle to your emotional body.

Certainly we could look at this circle many ways but lets simply see it as the emotional body now. I would suggest that it be gold as the suns rays are golden in nature because gold is an integrative color. It is radiating forth and then invoking from the cosmos the electrical magnetic response that will fulfill its desire to create, to be, to express. As you sense that radiation within that circle seek to see that as clearly as possible, the rays streaming from that center sun, streaming forth, filling the circle. Spend some time with that until you either see or know or both that is real for you. Now, the next part is the technique that I suggested.

Sense an electrical current coming into that whole circle, it may enter in any way that you wish, you could - and I am suggesting this possibility - see it as a lightning bolt coming into the circle, zig-zag it goes and it flashes into the circle. After three times of flashing it take a look at the circle. What has occurred? See what is there after the electrical current has entered through a light process - what has occurred as you bring the electrical magnetic energy into this radiant field that represents your emotional body. For some of you the field may no longer be cohesive - there may be gaps or spaces within it. The goal or we could say the ideal, is to now bridge any particular gaps or spaces that have been created.

You know the ideal - it is to have the cohesive light pattern as it was in the beginning - the energy field has become distorted through a particular response to a light/energy technique. If your field remains cohesive - does not separate - then there are no habit patterns in the sense that I have given them here in this material at this time, and you need do nothing else in this exercise.

If you find some spaces that have no radiance any longer then I suggest that you do the following: View now a spiral, it too is golden, and it spirals up, the base of the spiral will fit over the outside of your circle, it doesn't matter if you see it spiraling clock-wise or counter clock-wise because it isn't directional at all - it is the evolutionary process of Source. It is a light technique to evolve Sourceness. You place that then over your circle and you activate the spiral. Now it radiates through its activity, through its active state and as it does so it allows the energy field within your circle to heal. You can sense the spaces filling up, energy again becoming complete within the radiant field of your emotional body. Stay with the spiral until the field is complete. After you've done that I would rest a few minutes and then go through it all over again. Bring in your lightning bolts and see if your radiant field remains complete. If it does not, put your spiral back again. Now the spiral represents your Source's evolving point of view meaning that you are supported within the Source's evolving point of view and part of that support process is the ability to heal any points that become distorted in your own evolving understanding.

Now you may ask me "why do this - why create this incomplete field consciously?" with the lightning bolts. Well, the lightning bolts represent literally the same thing as the spiral except they represent your own electrical field or your ability to utilize the electrical magnetic energy of Source as a direct input to your creativity. Thus in a visualization you can see if you have built up an inappropriate amount of crystallization that shocks the system as electrical surges enter the emotional energy field.

To summarize then, a particular way of processing the emotional body becomes a bandaid that does not allow sometimes the complete healing that you wish, the point of origination which you cover up with the bandaid is never directly accessed. What I am suggesting is to view directly the whole energy field of your emotional responses exactly as they are bringing in a radiant stimulator - the lightning bolt- and seeing how cohesive is your response to this stimulation. Anything that is stimulative to your emotional body can create habit patterns thus the goal is to allow the emotional responses that you wish such as a loving, joyous response. Allow those positive responses to be "locked-in" if you will but deal with, in an ever evolving understanding, those responses that are not serving you well and that's of course what all of you are trying to do. My point is don't get locked into one system but vary the systems, progress them and then release the crystallization possibilities if you wish to utilize systems again that were habitual. It is easy to tell if there are habit patterns and the light and electrical system will help you heal those areas which are caught in this pattern of crystallization.

After you have worked extensively with any processing method, light techniques, light awareness, light understanding will allow you to accept and thus use the emotional body in a manner that is fully again the generative point of view which manifests through your heart. You have sought to connect into the heart center in an unlimited manner - your emotional body and the release of habitual patterns within it is the key for doing so.

USING A DODECAHEDRON FOCUS

I would like you to see now a Dodecahedron, Diagram #12, a twelve sided three dimensional figure. Visualize it structured by light, this structure rotates, again it doesn't matter which direction - it rotates - you get a sense then of its pulsing or its vibration; visually you can see its rotation and its pulse. Begin to view it, certainly see the whole dodecahedron, but focus slowly on each part of it - each section of light, going over it slowly from one side to the other until there is within you a sense of quality or balance of this rotating, pulsing light pattern. Sense the structural flow of light, the rhythmic pulsing of light into this chosen structure. Note its beauty, its simplicity, its balance and its ability to move, its life, and yet its stability. You may get a sense of transcendence and certainly the light flow within the dodecahedron intensifies the amount of light flowing, interacting, moving, pulsing within this light system. The light increases as you move in your awareness from one section to the other. Keep a balanced perspective as you move in your awareness from one point to the other, don't let go of the points that you've already viewed. You keep adding then other points into what already has been explored until you have explored in intimate detail the whole energy field of this dodecahedron.

Now after having completed the journey of exploring its parts I would like you to view it as whole, and then sense within you a radiance which allows you to center yourself within that dodecahedron. You become a centered point

DIAGRAM #12   DODECAHEDRON

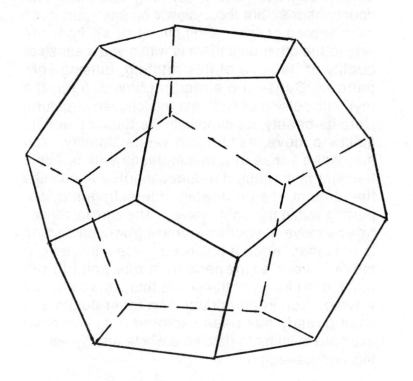

within it and that energy flows all around you. You are still aware of that energy as complete, each point has been explored comprehensively. Now, sense your radiance exploring each part of that dodecahedron and then in a reciprocal sense each part exploring your centered space. The energy flows out and flows in and you sense this full electrical pulsing system that you now know you are centered within and you recognize that without you at the center it would be incomplete because you are the means to process the incoming and the outgoing responses. Your centering is necessary to allow this process to be complete.

Doing this exercise will help you to grasp the creative process as a energized concept. The light structure shows you how creation comes about, at least through a structural or supportive point of view.

FREEING-UP THE FOUR BODY SYSTEM IN THE DIMENSIONS

Before you are Diagrams #13 A, B, &C which are meant to stimulate you. There are three of them and I suggest that you visualize the one that "speaks" to you first. Eventually it is suggested that you work with all of them but begin with the one to which your knowingness says "yes, I want to use this one first". You will establish then a means to open up your ability to utilize light technology. You approach it from your unique point of view, we could say that each one of these diagrams represents a door and because the room is round you can approach it from any door that you wish. Visualize the diagram you have chosen in front of you. It can be on a screen if you wish or, and this might be the most comprehensive way to work with this material, as a hologram, three dimensional. The goal for each of you is to understand and utilize the third dimension but not get stuck or caught in it. To progress your understanding of dimensions some of these diagrams will enhance your utilization of the dimensions, your ability to transcend, within the four body system, points where one or two of the bodies can't flow yet interdimensionally. Thus our exercises in this section are to free the four body system to express the many dimensions as you allow yourself to lighten the third dimension but not get stuck within it.

View then the diagram and view it as it is on the paper first - see it clearly - draw it over or follow each line until you have a sense of its proportion,

DIAGRAM #13 A - STRUCTURE #1

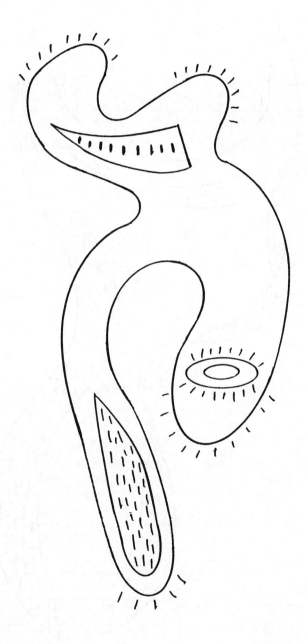

DIAGRAM #13 B - STRUCTURE #2

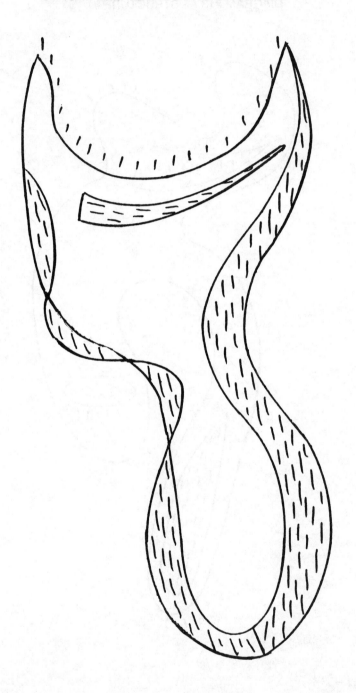

DIAGRAM #13 C - STRUCTURE #3

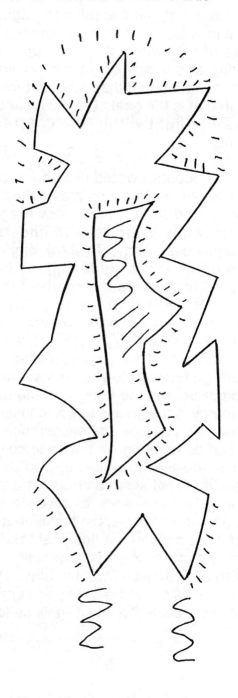

until the structure of the diagram vibrates or lights up. For some of you this will occur right away, for others it may take a little while before you can get a sense of light within this structure. It is worth persisting and it may be your knowingness that senses the light rather than a visual representation although that is the goal. But if your knowingness senses the light within the diagram that is sufficient.

When this occurs I would like you to sense that whole diagram melting, you create the image, you light it up and then it melts down again. The purpose of this exercise is to understand the creative process clearly. To show through a visual interpretation and a lightening technique that matter, whether we are talking about the physical plane or the state of being in its spiritual manifestation comes forth, lightens, and then is utilized as a means to create a flow into a new manifestation. Thus, as you melt down the structure go immediately in your visualization to the next structure and know that the first melted down energy is the means to get in touch with it as light also. As you view the second one you place the melted down energy or the life force that is now a flow into the second structure. You go over each line or part of that second structure until you can sense its light, its vibrancy, its alive state, and as it lights up more and more, the structure melts again and the light becomes a flow that takes you into the third structure. You sense that flow becoming that third structure so that it is alive. You again trace that third structure until you sense that life force at every point of it and it lights up for you. As

93

each structure then becomes light you sense that rather than its solid state. The solid state is transcended as you validate the structure as light but remember it has been formed from a light flow by transcending a previous structure so it has always been light but for a while the structure makes it appear solid.

You can utilize then all of these structures and I would suggest that you do and I would suggest that you create some of your own and utilize the same technique with them. Now, the next step it to ask yourself, your knowingness to visualize each of these structures within the different dimensions and do the same process. You've done it on the third dimension, do it on the fourth, fifth, and you can try it on the sixth dimension also. Thus you've seen each structure in the third now, ask your knowingness to visualize each structure on the fourth dimension until you have completed the whole series and then ask your knowingness to visualize it within the fifth dimension until you have completed the whole series and then within the sixth dimension until you have completed the whole series. Then go back and visualize each one as a third, fourth, fifth and sixth dimensional figure simultaneously, viewing then the third, fourth, fifth, and sixth as points upon a flow that you can view simultaneously. Go through the series in this manner. Note your responses to each part of this exercise and it may not be appropriate to sit down and do it all at once, I think perhaps that might overload the system just a little. This last one, the simultaneous flow of the third, fourth, fifth and sixth dimension as they relate to

each other, is important but should not be done
until you have done what precedes it. From this
one gains a sense of the true nature of structure as
a light supporting system that is not restricting but
the means to allow the light flow to keep
transcending itself.

You will note in the next Diagram #14A, the circles, one circle within another, within another, within another, and if you care to count them you will see there are nine circles. Visualize the nine circles and then rather like a folding telescope sense the center of the circle pulling away from you. The outside of the circle remains close but view the center of the circle as pulling away. A sense of movement from the center but you still remain focused with the outside circle. As the pulling away begins you sense that this is light, it is not solid, it is a light flow and it can flow eternally. There is a sense of light flow from that creative center that is going out and yet look - it is the center itself that is the flow. The outer circle is supportive of the flow but the flow is going out from the center. You know at this point that you are that center circle and you are moving, if you will, as light still aware or in contact with that outside circle or the support of the Whole and your awareness is both at that whole level and at the center of the circle that is ever flowing, ever moving, ever growing, in its light awareness.

Before you in Diagram 14B, is a triangle with its point up. This triangle is to be visualized in front of you. Now, this triangle is brown, a beautiful golden brown and it rests on the earth. See it there and it can be as large as you wish. Now as you bring it to the earth you can make it three dimensional and thus it literally becomes a pyramid. Now as you view it sense an emanation coming from it, a radiance, you know it is alive - there is life force

DIAGRAM #14A

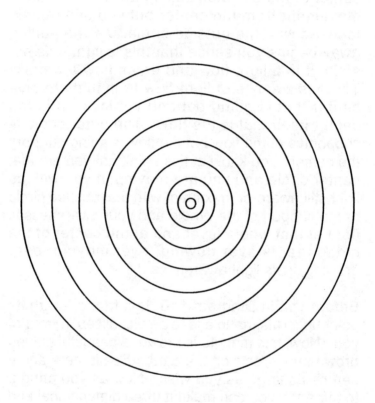

DIAGRAM #14B

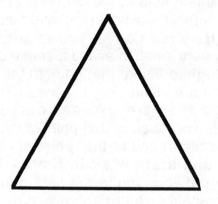

DIAGRAM #14C

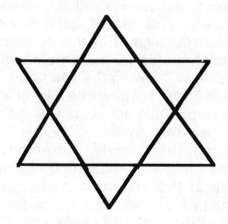

and that is golden in nature. Look at the point of the pyramid - there is a great deal of life force there because a centering process has taken place and the radiant field at the center is strongest of any point within the whole electrical field that this pyramid truly is. I'd like you to see yourself becoming very small in a visual sense or at least small enough to fit into that point of the pyramid. Now, if you are visualizing the pyramid as being very large then simply see yourself at the appropriate size to go to that point of the pyramid. Now the emanations at that point are so strong that you can literally sit in them. They are supportive of you, you're not sitting on a sharp point or anything, rather you are surrounded by these emanations that are coming from this triangle.

Now stretch out fully supported by the emanations and what you will notice is the approach from the cosmos of another triangle with its point coming toward you. It keeps coming, it is golden in color and its point is also very radiant. It approaches until it joins the radiant field that is supporting you from the other triangle. See that pyramid field stop at that point, no further movement until you feel comfortable in allowing the two fields to mingle more completely. There will be a lot of energy that this golden pyramid activates within the energy field of the brown pyramid. Sense the energy coming together slowly, remember you are supported - that will not change - by the energy structure of the brown pyramid but you are stimulated by the approach of the golden pyramid's radiance. When you are ready allow the golden pyramid to enter the structure of the brown pyramid until a Star of David shown in Diagram #14C is formed. Note where this places you. Your energy literally is a part now of the golden triangle. It is surrounded by the golden triangle and yet it remains supported by the brown triangle's radiance - that has not changed - but a Star of David has been formed and see where you are in that formation, allow that positioning if you will, to open up for you visually a sense of awareness of all of this structure as light.

In other words, as this Star of David manifests the pyramids light up. The coming together is what creates the light and one is no longer aware of the brown or the gold but simply that light interaction is creating a new structure that transcends the previous structure. The light has flowed and allowed a new structure to manifest. Several things may occur to you at this point. You may sense yourself becoming part of that light flow, identifying less and less yourself as you are, transcending individuality. If this does not occur you may sense a lot of energy within your physical body which responds or simply vibrates with this new structure. There may be other responses but as I view humanity it seems to me that these will be the most common responses, the ones most often expressed.

A sense then of being energized and sometimes transcending the individual responses is allowed by the joining together of two creative points that are symbolized here by the triangles. It really is talking about, of course, the spiritual piercing the physical, joining with it, lighting up and becoming a vehicle that enlarges and enhances both previous points of view.

ENERGIZING THE CHAKRAS WITH A BLUE ELECTRICAL STAR

View a five pointed star. It is blue and it is there before you. You have perhaps plucked it from the heavens and placed it there so you can view it. It is twinkling and shining and you sense that it literally has so much electrical life force that your viewing of it literally allows that energy that it contains to be reflected into your physical structure. You can bring that star as close as you wish. You can keep bringing it in closer and as you do its vibrant state will energize you more and more. I would suggest that you first place it in the crown chakra. After you have sensed the energy of the crown stimulated by it then see it entering the third eye chakra, now you can leave it in the crown also knowing that you are simply enlarging its use within your energy structure. After it has energized the third eye, continue its progression to the throat chakra and from the throat it will energize the heart and you know this is gently stimulating that area. Then move it to the solar plexus chakra - gently it balances this emotional center. Then move it to the polarity chakra where again a balancing of the male and female or the dynamic and receptive energies comes about through this star's energy. Then move it into the base or root chakra and you know this is stabilizing your foundation in its interaction with it. Then move it into the earth through your feet - open up the bottom of your feet and literally bring that star into the earth. See its energy spreading all over the earth. Then bring the earth response back up through your feet which will be - let us call it - the reverse side of the star. Its still the star but now on its opposite approach it comes up through your feet re-energizing the base, the polarity, the solar plexus, the heart, the throat, the third eye, and the crown. Then take it up to the eighth or the Soul Star chakra. Now as you do that, as you place it within the Soul Star sense the energy of the Whole coming into it also.

The energy goes out from it but the energy comes into the eighth chakra also. There is then a reciprocal flow that is blue and electrical in nature from the response at this eighth chakra level. Now as you visualize that sense that the eighth chakra becomes a structure that is everywhere, it is not just at the three inch above your head level but literally extends out from the body horizontally about five feet and then vertically extends all the way down into the earth. It is circular thus multi-directional going literally from every direction and to every direction. There is full motion, full reciprocal flow and it is balanced.

There is not an inappropriate directional flow but a multidirectional flow that is fully reciprocal, fully energized and fully supported by the incoming flow that surrounds it. Thus the generative point of existence itself is centered there stimulated at the eighth chakra and moves into a direction that becomes physical going through the seven chakras. It also enters a finer and finer energy formula going into the ninth, tenth, eleventh, and twelfth chakras also. Sense as it enters the ninth the full structure being energized, certainly there is an energy structure that goes out horizontally and goes out vertically that interacts with the energy structure that we have previously discussed. It then flows into the earth also. See then an energy structure at the tenth chakra level, it is horizontal and vertical, fully reciprocal and receives its support in a multi-directional flow manner. Certainly it is part of the column of light from the twelfth chakra and the eighth chakra but it is literally beyond a directional sense so it is stimulated literally from every point of view. Light interacting with light creating structure but then flowing to a new level to create from a different point of view a more encompassing structure and then finding itself responding to a stimulus from previous structure by melting down that previous structure and transcending it.

Thus we continue with the tenth, eleventh, twelfth chakras in the same manner sensing the flow of the structure but as we look now at this fully energized structure we become aware that the structure built at the lower levels or perhaps we could say at the crown chakra level is being transcended. That structure is changing and because it is changing there is a reverberating change that goes through all of the structures that have been built from it. Now, I did not direct your visualization of the structure through the system of the seventh chakras, the crown, the third eye and so forth in the same manner that we directed your visualization of the higher chakras and that is because on the physical level one is not as cognizant of light structure, at least for a while, but on the spiritual level or where the Soul Star is, the eighth chakra, one is aware of structural alignment.

Thus when we work to visualize at that level you can use the strength that resides on that level as a viewing port if you will. But, we can allow that level now, the eighth chakra Soul Star to show you visually the light structure available for you to see through the other seven chakras. Ask your soul then to show you the light structure that is present in the whole chakra system that has supported you on the physical plane.

Now remember, it is not just any point, it is a point that has energized a structural flow that you can view now and as you look at it in physicality it will seem directional, vertical and horizontal, and fully reciprocal in its flow. Energy points are created, moving and flowing. Each level is complete, each chakra level is complete and yet you will find that there are connecting points between the chakras, points of flow connection that allow each structure to be a part of a much larger structure. Sense then, as much as you can, each level's structure, in other words, begin with the crown and get a sense of it. Now, if you wish, remain focused physically, in other words, sense that you have a physical body but that this energy flow surrounds it to begin with. In other words, see the structural support system that is there within your energy field at the crown chakra level, begin to glimpse it with your knowingness. It still seems that you have a solid body - that's all right. You can glimpse the structural flow that can also be viewed as an adjacent area to the physical dense plane. That's one way to view it. However, as you progress your understanding let go of the need to see a physical dense body but recognize that this flow is that point that you have considered dense matter and as it now flows through this electrical support system, each level connected to the next level, each point a stimulating point within the Whole, that you are constantly renewing at a different level your understanding of life. Thus the physical level matter is always being transcended in your understanding that what you have called solid is not, it is a flow - it has movement - it is energy.

Now, it is important to allow yourself to develop this awareness of the body as energy, the energy can be seen, it is visual, it is light. It has the capacity to transcend itself. As you first view your levels of life force or energy as the structural connections from a point that we call a chakra center and begin to see how they are connected at every point with another level it is necessary to brighten that energy perspective by seeing that at certain points in your evolution you bring in to your awareness a cosmic stimulator or a light focus which shows you ever more clearly this creative process and how to transcend the point where you are now. Your energy structure becomes then a ladder, literally Jacob's Ladder, that you utilize to expand your awareness and to see that flow is all there is and it is a light flow of electrical magnetic energy that explores ever more completely as it gains and regains a sense of who it is.

THE "V" FOCUS

Visualize a very large "V" and zero in or focus in on the point where the two arms of the "V" join - the center - now as you broaden your perspective you are viewing the "V" not only in front of you but you are looking down at it and viewing that point so that a vertical view of the "V" as well as a horizontal view of the "V" is possible. You can look horizontally, vertically and a combination - you really have an all encompassing view of that "V". In point in fact, the "V" begins to rotate and spins faster, and faster, and faster, and faster, and faster - you have a sense of the center of the "V" as the pivotal point around which all of this movement now occurs. Now, sense that "V" as light, a light focus that is movement and yet has a center that you can view from any point that you wish. That centering is there as a stabilizing factor within the movement of the light. As you view it then enter that point with your awareness - become aware of yourself as centered there. Now, streaming in to you from every point of view which the movement of the "V" arms represent is light and we could color this light and say that a rainbow of colors is coming in. What you sense is a rainbow because of the movement. Light becomes color as the movement of the light or the flow of the light identifies for you particular characteristics of the light. Each ingredient of light has a particular color and you sense that as the "V" spins it is a rainbow and that rainbow comes into that point of centering where you are. This exercise - staying within that spinning rainbow - is a stabilizer and if you feel you need to be stabilized it is a good technique to utilize. You can do it as often and really as long as you wish. And it will work to stabilize the four body system. It will help to align the system and to make available to you a concept of wholeness and the transcending of specifics that have not seen the whole picture.

STEPPING ON LIGHT

View yourself walking on a path of light. We could say it is a road that is lit up. It is transparent but what you see through it is simply more light so it is an intense light that you are walking on. As you walk on it the light isn't solid so you sink into the light. Now it seems very supportive even if you are sometimes knee deep in light - sometimes you don't sink in that much. You can begin to dance on this light - whatever kind of dance you wish - begin to dance on it - now you will note something interesting. If you turn around and look at the path where you have been, you have left footprints there, footprints in the light and you know that your unique footprints are a permanent part now of that light. You've changed the light by stepping on it. What you are has created a difference in the light, not in an inappropriate sense but your footprints or your dance has now become a part of what that light is. Now, of course you recognize that the footprints from everyone that has ever been and ever will be walking in the light blend. And if you look closely you will see coming toward you someone else on that light path and their footprints sometimes enlarge your footprints creating a unique pattern in the light that is beyond what either one of you could create. Your footprints have now joined to create a unique interpretation of light expression. The little one comes up to you and asks you to dance and the two of you continue down the path dancing together creating unique footprints together, a cosmic light dance indeed. View then a much larger road that all humanity dances on. It is a light path right here on the

107

physical plane. All of humanity dancing together on it. Can one dance on a path of light if you are not yet aware of self as light? Of course. There are levels of self that are aware of it in everyone thus we are talking about a cosmic dance in which the soul level participates fully, willingly and creatively.

However, on the physical plane your permission is needed to grow in awareness of how to use the physical plane's expression in a more comprehensive manner. In other words, your physical point of view must willingly allow itself to recognize light. When it does so the path that is physical joins the path that is spiritual. The coming together unites and expands the path, it becomes a very cosmic perspective and yet the focus of it, for a while anyway, remains physical. It takes with it eternally what has been gained on the physical plane. The cosmic dance of light is chosen by all aspects of self allowing the footprints to reflect an awareness that light is an interaction of creative possibilities with all levels, all aspects, all potentialities. The more that is realized the lighter the path, the more comprehensively one dances, the greater the perspective of light comes forth.

WEAVING THE GARMENT OF LIGHT

I'd like you to see before you a loom, one that you can weave on, and you have a ball of a material like yarn only yours is light and you have your consciousness as the means to weave with it. Now you can create a design using specific colors which are aspects of light. You can design what you wish to create but keep it in mind that when you get it created you are going to wear it rather as a garment of light. So how would you like to design a garment to wear as your body of light - what colors would you like? Do you want a particular design? whatever you wish - begin to weave it now. You might want to sit down and draw it on a piece of paper - what sort of a design? Now it will fit over your physical structure - that's not really the way it is but that's close enough for our analogy here.

So after you have woven it I invite you to put it on. Put on your body of light in your awareness, fit it on, get it smooth so that it fits over the physical structure, get it smooth and then look at your physical structure - view it with your knowingness or your third eye or a combination of both. View it now - how magnificent, how radiant you are. Now know this is a permanent garment you have put on so you might want to see how beautiful you can make it. It is permanent. Now the good news is you can keep refining your understanding of it and although the light garment is permanent you can see it in an ever more refined manner. Colors are viewed one way one time and then another way another time until you are aware of color but the overall effect is simply the whole spectrum of light. So after you create your light garment and put it on then get in touch with it in each part of the physical body refining your understanding. Look under your toenails and under your fingernails and see the light. See it radiate where your hair is, see it go beneath your skin.

In other words, your physical body is a component of light so we are not going to take away the physical body especially, we are going to know that we may see the physical body either as you see it now, in its solid state, or as light. So see where the light fits into the physical structure, look at the light in your liver, look at it in your pancreas, certainly look at it in your heart, look at it in the tissue of your body, look at it in the blood flow of your body, look at it in the dermis, look at it in the blood vessels themselves, look at it in the bones - the bone marrow, look at it in the meridians, look at it in the joints, look at it now at the cellular level which is a radiant core for the physical structure, look at it in your teeth, your eyes and your ears, look at the light all over - this is what you have put on - your tongue, your lips, your cheeks, the skin itself - each point as light. Radiant, alive, the body of light manifested on the physical plane - the more completely you do this, the more real it is for you; the sooner you will allow yourself to see the reality of existence - that all is light. Look at yourself in the mirror - see light.

Begin by looking around your physical body - see the radiant emanations of the auric field. Then consciously superimpose the light onto the physical structure, allow it, the light, to penetrate into the physical structure or you to see it that way going to a deeper and deeper level within the physical structure. Start at the outside with the skin and then move below the skin going ever deeper until you reach an awareness that you've penetrated or seen the light penetrate until it literally comes out the other side again as light. Light on every level of the physical, a radiant light being, you've seen yourself as you really are. The first time that you do this spend enough time with it that you get a sense of the presence of light within you - as much as you can - the more often you do it, the more consistently you seek to view yourself as light the better. And then view others and other objects, everything as light, sense as much as you can the light of all that is.

An analysis of light, of your light, will show you that certain aspects of self have accepted more light than other aspects. Light is not gained uniformly, but in bursts and spurts is light accepted and evening out the flow of the acceptance is important. If, in your life, there is a period where there is confusion and others do not seem to communicate with you clearly and you with them then a certain aspect of self is not yet allowing the light to show up within it. A part of you is resisting the light. Generally it is the emotional body but the physical body also may have patterns of resistance to the light thus I wish to share with you now a particular pattern of behavior of light resistance because of an event in your planet's history. There are cosmic events which create effects in physical existence. In your sequencing of time then on the physical plane eons ago when your earth was very young a cosmic event occurred which created a light alignment for the Source level which multiplied the light many times. The Source then merged with a greater point of awareness and became greater because of entering with this clearer perspective. Two levels came together and became greater because of it. This is the most recent joining of Source and is not truly a major joining point, there are several major joining points and this is rather a minor one comparatively speaking but it certainly is the most recent joining of Source in a sequential sense.

Now let us say that you are a youngster, a child let us say, a child about six years old and your father and mother have been married longer than you have lived so you have a mother and a father but your mother is no longer around - we won't speculate why. There's been a change and your father tells you he's going to be married again. Well, you've had one type of guidance system with your natural mother and your father, you are going to have another type of guidance system as your father marries again. Let us say that your parents were only moderately compatible but that your father relates to his new wife in a way that he never related to your mother, there is such a compatibility factor that its very obvious your father has expanded, has grown, is much happier and the life shows it.

Can you see how you as a six year old might get mixed feelings and messages here? Your mother is no longer here but someone else is and because your father is very happy with this new joining it is obvious that it is a productive new beginning but remember you are very young - only six - and you're still feeling the loss of your mother. You get a mixed message then - a loss and yet the happiness of your father and the expansion because of his happiness are very clear to you also. This could be an example within a person's life but the example that I'm truly giving you is within your planet's life.

Your planet then has a particular guidance system and through a joining, a merging, at a higher level where your planetary consciousness could not perhaps follow, it was too young to comprehend what was going on, there was a very encompassing change - it literally changed the way the support system of your planet came forth after that. There was a change in the administrative linkage system of your planet. Literally the light within that administrative link became brighter and the little planet knew it was basically very productive but it also felt a great deal of loss of what had been. A mixed message then came to the little planet. Now keep in mind this is the environmental pattern that each of you live in. We are talking literally here now about the all encompassing consciousness level or what has been termed the mass consciousness.

Remember I have already stated to you before that the mass consciousness is not negative. Certainly it contains some specific beliefs that are not serving it well but the mass consciousness of your planet is the overall awareness pattern that all of the kingdoms feed into it and that is reflected from higher levels into it so it is not negative. The reason I'm stating that is that there are those of you that believe you should get rid of any association with the mass consciousness but truly what you are trying to seek to do is to get rid of connections into the mass consciousness that are specifically patterns or beliefs that are not productive - fear patterns or loss patterns. Thus we have seen a specific pattern that occurred early in your planets history becomes now an opposition pattern as each of you seek to allow a great expansion of light. As your guidance system grows greater than your connection into the mass consciousness this specific pattern states that a great loss is now occurring. I would suggest that through some sort of a method you begin to release the beliefs that you contact in this regard. Certainly a very valid approach would be to put some specific affirmations into a lake, I've given you, already, in another section of this material how to utilize the lake of the subconscious and following now are a few affirmations to help you in regard to what we have just seen here as a part of a behavioral pattern attachment into the mass consciousness. See your lake a specific color then and slide in the following:

I ACCEPT THIS EXPANDED GUIDANCE SYSTEM THAT COMES TO ME NOW ON THE PHYSICAL LEVEL.

I CAN SEE THE EXPANSION OF MY GUIDANCE SYSTEM AND I ACCEPT IT NOW WITHOUT OPPOSITION, WITHOUT FEAR, WITHOUT LOSS .

I ACCEPT THIS EXPANSION KNOWING THAT MY GUIDANCE SYSTEM HAS ALLOWED IT TO OCCUR NOW.

ALLOWINGINESS IS UTILIZED BY ME TO CONNECT INTO THE EXPANDED AWARENESS SYSTEM WHICH INCREASES MY ABILITY TO UTILIZE LIGHT ON THE PHYSICAL PLANE NOW.

ALL IS LIGHT AND I RECOGNIZE THERE IS NO RESISTANCE TO EMBODYING THAT LIGHT NOW ON THE PHYSICAL PLANE.

MY SOUL ACCEPTS THE LIGHT AND I ACCEPT THE CLEAR GUIDANCE OF MY SOUL ON THE PHYSICAL PLANE NOW.

ALL RESISTANCE TO THE ACCEPTANCE OF THIS WIDENING PERSPECTIVE CALLED MY GUIDANCE SYSTEM IS GONE, THE PHYSICAL LEVEL IS ACCEPTING THIS ENLARGED GUIDANCE NOW.

THE ENLARGED PERSPECTIVE WHICH GUIDES ME IS ALLOWED TO COME FORTH ONTO THE PHYSICAL PLANE NOW.

I RELEASE ALL RESISTANCE TO ACCEPTING FROM THE SPIRITUAL PLANE THIS ENLARGED GUIDANCE SYSTEM NOW.

THE LIGHT OF MY SOUL IS ACCEPTING ALL ENLARGEMENTS OF A DIVINE GUIDANCE SYSTEM WHICH SUPPORTS MY PHYSICAL LIFE NOW.

See yourself on a slide, the slide is golden and you know that as you go down it you are going to land in some energy. Now, see yourself sliding down the slide, landing in some energy and see what color it is and where you land, in other words, there is a circle of energy that you land in - do you land in the center, are you off center, more to the left or the right, whereabouts do you land? As you sense where you land draw that out onto a piece of paper and also the color of the energy. Do this six times until you have six circles of energy all together as a circle. You see six small circles that make up a large circle. You will give each circle a color as you note it from landing in it and you will also place a dot in each circle as to where you landed. Then look at your six circles, see the colors that are coming together and also see where the dots are that you have drawn as a landing focus. What sort of figure geometrically do you get from your six dots? What does your knowingness say about it? Now, after you've looked at it as much as you can, I'd like you to see a white light literally coming into the six circles and moving the dots around, actually they melt into the circle. But then, after they melt, a new dot will be formed. See what position that new dot takes within the circle.

Do this for each circle. You will allow the light to light up all six circles at once but look individually at each circle to see where the new dot has formed and after you've done that with all six look again at what geometric figure is given by the lighting up of the six circles. What has happened to the color also in each one. What you are seeking to do is see what difference lighting up this creative effort that you've landed in has made.

Now, this exercise is really signifying landing within the mass consciousness; different aspects of the mass consciousness, each one will be given a color, you will need then to ask your knowingness what each color represents within the mass consciousness and I feel that this will be a unique perspective for each of you. Not necessarily in line with any sort of a color system at all but red might mean to you anger you see, that wouldn't be too unusual, while for some of you yellow may be excitability but I can see how for some others of you yellow may mean tranquility. There is quite a bit of difference in the use of color within the mass consciousness.

Now, the point of doing this is to identify with the specific ways you are connected into the mass consciousness and to seek to see how to uniformly lighten up the perspectives, the connections that are not serving you well in that area. Whatever it is then, take a look at it and see if there is something within each one of these symbols as you understand it from the color perspective you've given it and from the dot position you've given it and then in relationship to the other circles. This is an exercise in lighting up your relationship with the mass consciousness and seeking to understand something from doing so. It would be appropriate to work with this exercise once in a while to keep lighting it up and keep re-energizing it to see what you can learn about what you believe in relationship to the mass consciousness.

Now you can do this as many times as you want. Each time you go down the slide and land into that circle of energy it will represent then sliding into the mass consciousness and you will perhaps from what your consciousness has been doing, from what you are focused in at that particular time guide the colors that you see and your awarenesses about what that particular circle is. So it is a good way to see as you learn and you grow what is going on right then in your relationship with the mass consciousness.

Now, if you are in a personal relationship and let us say you have an argument with your relationship partner as you try to figure out how to clear that a good technique is to use a slide, land in your circle and see how your mass consciousness relationship is affecting you. Let me give you an example:

After an argument with your relationship partner see yourself going down the slide and landing in the circle of energy and that energy is brown and you land clear over in the right hand corner let us say, right near the edge of the circle, then it seems to me that what we have here we will relate the brown color to the earth and literally that positioning and that color is saying "I feel closed out of life rigidly by this physical relationship that is taking away my ability to be balanced in my life, I still am here but I'm pushed into the corner by it and it is on the physical plane that I feel pressured now." Now, you may not, for a while, be able to get that comprehensive an awareness from working with these circles but each time you seek to

118

analyze it I would like you to do it this way: - You've gone down the slide - you've landed in your circle - you've seen that it is brown - and you see that you've landed over by the border of the circle. Now, turn on a lamp, you know it is a Source lamp, turn on that light into the circle. It will allow you to see it more clearly and to have your knowingness from a very basic level of your beingness guide your understanding so that you may more clearly interpret what this exercise is seeking to convey to you. A communication with this exercise is necessary. You can personify it enough so that it can really talk to you, allow your circles to talk to you - ask it "what's going on "? - if it says "I don't know," then keep questioning it in various ways until you get to a part that it does know because it does, you just simply have to keep moving around in your questions until you come to a way that it can respond to you.

It is important to see this relationship with the mass consciousness and how it is affecting the daily activities of your life. I feel that this technique can be helpful to you. Now let us say that you absolutely cannot get very much out of it the first time that you do it. Each circle seems not very clear to you - why you've landed where you did and why the color that it is - you can ask all of the circles to, let us say, communicate to you in an integrated manner. You can have a communicative link with that Whole perspective. Let us say you've asked and you haven't found out anything - now you're asking for a unified reply and you may get "well, the whole question involves unity - it involves being integrated and there is confusion from one circle to the next - one pulling me out of balance and the next pushing me and pressuring me. There's no way to bring it all together." Again, I suggest that at these points where there seems to be resistance in the evolution, whether it is in this exercise or in your life that these light techniques of really lighting up the situation, can be very helpful.

See now at the Source level an opening a connection at that Source level which can, for this exercise, be the most brilliant point that you can imagine. Certainly the Source level is all encompassing but let's say that a point where you can connect into is being envisioned as a brilliant point that is absolutely the most brilliant point you can imagine. Then sense that brilliance, that energy really flowing now into these six points, lighting them up and allowing a communication between the points to tell you what is going on. Now, you create, if you wish, a little play. Ask your aspects - the six circles - to write a little story and give you a symbolic way of looking at the exercise. Then ask the six aspects or the six circles to assume a role, a story and learn from it. An example might be: you see them as six children. What are the doing? What are they into emotionally? What are they into physically? What are they beginning to realize spiritually? And so on. Certainly I'm not leaving out the mental body but in the case of these children it is probably, at the point where we are now, not the mental body that is resistive. It is probably the emotional, the physical or perhaps the spiritual connection that is involved here. Now in the circles there may be some reluctance to use the mental body but usually in a symbolic exercise such as this it is the spiritual connection that is being stretched, enlarged and the emotional response that needs to feel secure and sometimes a letting go on the physical plane that is being utilized now.

This exercise can be very important and I would state to use your creativity, really ask these six circles to reply to you and imagine that they are replying and then listen to what they say and if they give you only a few words write those down and then later you can put together a little more clearly what those words mean. But begin to feed into an evaluation system, gradually, so that you will be able to assess where you are in your allowing of more light to be your guidance system.

ADDING LIGHT TO THE BODY

As one makes light connections there are ways to lessen any residue of resistance, to not be affected by the remnants of old patterns that have still some hold over you. One of the most important techniques is the conscious placement of light within the physical structure. To see yourself as light, to visualize yourself as light. You can't do this too often, the more often you do it - the better! The more intensely you do it - the better. The more you do it specifically into various parts of the physical structure - the better. In other words, specifically add the light to your heart, specifically to your throat, specifically to the bowel area for example, to the brain area, to the back area, to the head area in general. In other words, a light enhancement where you envision the physical structure as light will allow an absorption of what that light symbolizes into your awareness.

The reason then, for bringing in more light is to allow yourself to access wholistic creativity, the light represents wholeness. That is why it is so important. It is a symbol of wholeness, a symbol of the integrative understanding that all of you are seeking which manifests the Co-Creator level. You can't have a Co-Creator level without all encompassing light and you can't enter all encompassing light without manifesting the Co-Creator level. They go together, they are the same but you might say the Creator has built into the system your relating to light and your attraction to it for the very purpose of bringing you an opportunity to enter the co-creator level. It seems attractive to you and the light then is sought by you, but at this point some of you don't understand why.

This is the same type of reasoning that brings a man and a woman together in a sexual attraction. What they create from this attraction is often a new beginning of creativity come forth from an attraction that is not yet complete in its understanding but even if it isn't it accomplishes the goal that it sets out to accomplish and that's important. Your more limited understanding does not limit your use of light, you can use light levels and contact awareness levels that are much greater than you consciously can recognize. You can use these levels as a creative stimulus that allows you, although focused at a less comprehensive level, to begin a process of releasing old patterns by stimulating the cosmic equivalency of what your limited consciousness can yet envision. You see, you are connected to that very basic Source level and it really isn't above and below, you know that, it is literally - while you are on the physical plane - an inner and an outer perspective or a contact into the heart center is perhaps the clearest way of putting it but you can use your present point of view which is rather limited, particularly while you are here on the physical plane, to accomplish a very comprehensive creating indeed.

Just as a child is born through sexual activity which can be rather limited in its understanding you give birth to a creativity level that can be very cosmic indeed but is only beginning to understand that cosmic potentiality. It is necessary to perhaps acknowledge that this is the beginning of much. The amount of cosmic awareness that you have invested through a light connection will stimulate on the physical plane the use of this light connection and will allow the cosmic and physical points of view to join together and when that occurs indeed there is a cosmic beginning, an unfoldment that literally the angelic hosts celebrate because it is that coming together that we call the beginning of the embodiment of the co-creator level. Everything comes together, everything wakes up, everything lights up, everything is sorted out, everything flows, all points of view then come into perfect alignment and gain a cosmic brilliance that shines throughout the universe.

THE GOLDEN BALL

See a golden ball of energy. Now you can throw it in front of you or behind you. If you throw it in front of you it goes into an area with blue energy and thus it bounces back to you blue. If you throw it behind you there is no telling what color it will come back. You throw it out from behind and it goes a little further than if you throw it ahead of you. And it comes back a particular color. So now throw in front of you it comes back a beautiful blue, - then throw it out behind you and see what color comes back. Place whatever color it came back with inside a blue framework. So now you have a particular color with a beautiful, iridescent blue framework and sense the center literally melting. The particular color that you saw in the center is melting and as it melts it runs into the beautiful blue and sense what is occurring within the blue that is surrounding it. Sense that, allow it and know that the two colors coming together are really stimulative of something and seek through your knowingness to see what is being stimulated there.

You know then that this exercise is to stimulate something within your creativity. What is being stimulated now? Go within and then see, ask your knowingness and sense an expanded awareness from having done so, sense an ability to clearly ascertain your awareness of what this symbol means now. As you begin to allow yourself to use these light techniques it will become more and more clear that you are simply utilizing the light technology that is flowing all around you to become more aware. You are cleaning up your act in regard to light, if you will, being stimulated by particular light focuses, recognizing that this stimulation can clean up specific remnants that may have been there for a while but you couldn't or wouldn't get rid of them. I have a few affirmations to put in the lake in case you don't want to give up one of these energy remnants. Get your lake, a particular color then and slide in the following:

I ACCEPT THIS ENERGY NOW KNOWING THAT I HAVE NOT LOST OR RECEIVED AN ADVERSE EFFECT FROM DOING SO.

THERE IS NO NEED TO DISRUPT THE FLOW OF ENERGY THAT IS COMING TO ME THROUGH THIS LIGHT PERSPECTIVE. I ALLOW IT NOW.

THERE IS A GOOD JOINING HERE AND I ACCEPT THE CLEAR EFFECTS WHICH ARE MANIFESTING THROUGH THIS JOINING NOW.

THERE IS NO DISRUPTIVE PATTERNING IN THIS JOINING PROCESS. IT COMES TOGETHER NOW.

I ALLOW THE ALL ENCOMPASSING LIGHT TO BE PRESENT IN MY LIFE. I ACCEPT COMPLETE INTEGRATION FROM ALLOWING IT NOW.

ENERGIZING GOALS BY BREAKING UP CRYSTALLIZED PATTERNS

This is an exercise which I suggest you do which will break up old crystallization patterns through a light technique, and energize an opportunity or goal.

See yourself walking down a corridor. There are doors on both sides of the corridor and as you walk you know you are going to make choices. You will walk to a particular door and open it. Note if it is on the right or the left. Go to that particular door and open it. Now the goal is to learn from this perspective that you've chosen. There will be a symbolic experience that you will gain through this door but first of all, before you open the door, as you stand there before it, through your third eye project light right through the door because light is not stopped by a door. Project light through the door as much as you can. Sense light flooding into that symbolic experience that you are about to enter. Allow about two minutes of projection here and you might want to use a clock to show you that at least two minutes has gone by. Two minutes of projecting the light into this experience and then open the door. You will have a symbolic experience which you will interpret much as you do a dream using the same sort of symbology that one uses in a dream.

Remember if you see other people then in connection with your experience one way to interpret it is to see all people as a part of yourself. In this experience, however, because it is a light projection experience other people may also represent other parts of the plan or other people as they interact with you so it will be necessary to interpret from several points of view, a wholistic point of view rather than just from a personal point of view where you play all of the roles in this symbolic experience. I feel you will gain then through this light enhancement an ability to interpret both what is going on in your life beyond what you consciously recognize at this point and also to see into your relationship with others in a way that is currently beyond your own ability to view it. Can you see then that a projection of light held into an opportunity lights up that opportunity, energizes it with the light that has a magnetic attraction to bring through that opportunity all of your potential or to allow that opportunity to energize your potential and help you create it. I would suggest then as a progression of this exercise that whenever you know very clearly what you want in your life and I say that very carefully - that you stand before the door to it, project light through that door into that opportunity to energize it before you enter a relationship with it.

Let me give you an example. Many of you are seeking full abundance. I would say that it is important to know what sort of resistance you are holding in that area and unless you are currently allowing an unlimited flow right now you do have some resistance and it is important to keep searching for that to see why it is there and what it is exactly. But be cognizant then that what you will energize can also be any resistances that are attached to the area you are trying to enter. Now, does this mean that you shouldn't use this technique? Of course not. But it can mean that you will not overuse the technique. I have stated to project the light through for two minutes - that's about the right amount. Do not sit there for 20 or 30 minutes projecting the light into this opportunity or you may find you have put so much energy into the resistance part that you will have greater difficulty in connecting than if you hadn't done the exercise at all. In other words my friends, utilize all of these techniques in a balanced manner. If particular guidance is given by me in the ways to use them, know this, I am not just arbitrarily giving you some rules, I have seen, perhaps a little clearer than you can yet see, how to use these techniques in a balanced manner. The reason for this guidance is I've seen some of you use affirmations when there is so much resistance in an area that what you are really affirming is the resistance because you are not yet cognizant of how to utilize in a balanced way techniques that attract what is desired or the ideal without putting so much energy into what is yet being resisted that it becomes even more difficult to get what you wanted then before.

The technique of the lake is one of the most effective uses of affirmations that I have seen as I see how it works now within many of you that are using it. The reason is this: it places the affirmation in a visual sense right within the flow of the subconscious. It softens then the resistance before the resistance becomes too solid. It is then a direct means of softening resistance so to avoid the affirmation of the resistance over and over as you affirm the clearer point of view. I would say, unfortunately, however, because in your past lives you've all used affirmations many of you have rather a lot of resistance in certain areas. That is why, in the Foundation, we began with patterns - breaking up these crystallized points, in order to release the levels or resistance that have become frozen or crystallized over your many lives on the earth. It would not have occurred if you had not overdone the use of affirmations. Be aware then that there are many, many good techniques and certainly the light techniques are very helpful but be also aware that using them in the way that I have instructed you is the balanced approach to using them.

FINDING A KEY IN THE LIGHT

This is another light technique: See yourself sitting in front of a beautiful fire. Light a campfire and it flares up. The light is beautiful. The fire glows and burns brightly. It doesn't burn down it stays constant and as you look deep into the flames you begin now to see a particular image. Now this image will bring you a symbol, a symbol that comes out of the flames and the light and this symbol that you summon from the flames and the light will identify for you a particular key which allows you to integrate or put together or comprehend the various situations in your life and allows you to know how the light aspect of self can make a difference in integrating these parts of your life. The symbol will talk to you. It will speak both by what it is and if you wish words can flow to you from it. It may glow and radiate - sense its size, its shape, its color, what it says, its attitude, its function, its position, in other words, gain as you gaze at the flames as comprehensive an awareness about what the flame, the light, is bringing you as possible.

Plan to spend 20 to 30 minutes with this exercise. Now, that's quite a while and the exercise will progress and possibly you will no longer see the symbol as coming out of the flame. Allow it then to evolve but know that the basis of the flame and the light has built the perspective that you are now getting. Many times such a light connection will identify for you some very important points that can be communicated only through light. The comprehensive stimulus that such a light technique can bring to you is almost awesome. It will be best to do this exercise when you are feeling quite balanced. If you are not balanced and it doesn't flow well I would suggest that you use other light techniques to get back in balance at first and then come back to this exercise again. What you look for then is a particular symbol within the light flow and then the progression to you of what that symbol means. This is really comprehensively entering the light and discovering through a particular focus what lies there for you. An awakening then through a light focus will begin for you. Some of you will discover some rather awesome material within this light. Remember this is a very magnetic, very dynamic point of contact and can show you rather comprehensively many, many things.

LIGHTING UP COMMUNICATION

This is another technique: You have before you a book and you also have a giant flashlight. I invite you to open the book to any page that your knowingness tells you to and then shine your flashlight on the page and read it. You may want to write down or tape what is written on that page. The light connection can show you what specific page you have chosen to read in the awareness connection that we are calling a book. Literally what you will get here is some communication from a higher perspective of self that is seeking to light up your life or seeking to show you how to light up your life thus you will get some helpful suggestions by using this technique. You may, of course, look at as many pages as you wish but be sure to light each one up and you might spend a moment or two lighting it up rather comprehensively before you begin to read it. The more light, up to a balanced point - remember - that you put into the connecting effort, the better you will be able to read it. Light always allows a connection to be perceived. That is the very nature of light - it shows a connection.

GETTING IN TOUCH WITH THE RHYTHM OF EXISTENCE

I'd like you to see a giant clock and it has a pendulum and it moves back and forth, tick-tock, tick-tock, tick-tock; now as the pendulum swings in the tick it contacts a point and that point lights up so the tick is light and then it moves to the tock and as it contacts that lights up. Tock/LIGHT, tick/LIGHT, tock/LIGHT, tick/LIGHT, tock/LIGHT; there is a contact with LIGHT as the rhythm of existence flows. Sense the lighting up of the flow through this rhythm. As you sit and watch your clock sense what occurs as you allow yourself to be consciously a part of this rhythm tick/LIGHT, tock/LIGHT, tick/LIGHT, tock/LIGHT, tick/LIGHT, tock/LIGHT. The LIGHT is indeed created through the rhythm of existence as it flows and interacts with other levels which have rhythmic divine patterns within them also. As you become aware of this rhythm there is an emphasis of LIGHT so that each time you hear a clock - you begin to think LIGHT. Every time you hear some music - the rhythm - you begin to see and think LIGHT. Sense then the connection between divine rhythm and the creation of LIGHT. They come together through your conscious recognition that they are together. There is an identification process that says this is the divine rhythm and therefore LIGHT is created. Can you see then that you establish a relationship within your subconscious mind, within that creative vehicle that says "Look! That is rhythm and therefore that is LIGHT".

134

Before you are screens and they are rather like a movable blackboard. You can move them around any way you wish and there are ten of them. They are transparent and you know that if you get all ten lined up correctly what you're going to get is that whole white light that you are seeking. Now, some screens are green, some are blue, some are red, some are yellow, various colors - you've got ten of them. Now there is in the distance a spotlight that is shining from that point beyond the screens back at you but you can't see it yet because you haven't aligned your ten light screens.

They are very easy to move around. I want you to move them around until they are aligned so completely that you can sense that light pouring through them. Spend some time with it - you've got ten. Just move them, shift them and when you get them all lined up then look at that light shining back to you now. Sense then how it feels and what it looks like to have that light alignment. You have the aspects aligned so that there is a crystal clear light presence that is shining back at you. This again is a visual technique to help you in lining up the aspects so that your subconscious vehicle can recognize that that is the goal - the alignment of all aspects into this crystal clear energy vehicle that we call light.

One begins to sense then through light exercises or techniques the availability of complete integration. In point of fact, that is why we suggest that you utilize light techniques as it keeps creating a clearer understanding, a clearer perspective until that all encompassing clear point is reached in your awareness which we call the manifested co-creator level. Light technology and the use of it is truly in a cosmic sense only beginning on your planet, but it is beginning. You will find within the media, within advertising ranks those that have pulled, perhaps not yet consciously, but pulled from the universal mind the importance of light technology and are using it to advertise because they recognize how magnetic light technology is and how appropriately it reaches into the buying public's creativity and desire nature. One way to see the evolution of your planet is to watch the advertisements in your media. Certainly you must be aware of what you are looking for and certainly you must sort out the patterned responses from the clear responses but one thing that is overwhelmingly clear now is your planet has a greater awareness of light and the electrical effects of light and the stimulative effects of light and the radiant effects of light. Thus in an attempt to draw sales from humanity the advertisers are utilizing the light technology and the media responds to it by seeing, not yet clearly, but identifying certain aspects of it and commenting on them.

Until however, you look at the spiritual point of view, you do miss or are not able to put together the complete framework within which the events on earth fit. There isn't any way to see them clearly until you go beyond the physical level but it is obvious to all of us, your spiritual friends, that light awareness is multiplying rapidly on the earth. We see it in the sparkle and shine within your civilization, especially the Western civilization but we also see it as a settling effect in the Eastern civilization, not the religious sects but those in the Eastern civilizations that have had difficult lives or have been very poor or that have almost turned off an awareness of survival on the physical plane are settling in through this lighting perspective in a way which allows their lives to be a little easier.

Truly, all of humanity is benefitting from the light technology that is already flowing within the mass media. Not that you can see, necessarily, the connection that I am speaking of, if you try to connect the advertisements into an affect but what you will see is the masses of those that are "poor" having just a little bit of an easier time. I think it will take about nine months before that is very obvious. We on a spiritual plane can see it more clearly - on the physical plane it is perhaps not yet noticed. Remember, we are talking about a slight lessening and that is the way evolution takes place - one step at a time - people learn to release and as they learn to release they allow a new beginning.

After that new beginning is energized very well it allows a progressive understanding from what that new beginning has been or the bringing of more light allows a penetration into an understanding as never before. It is important then to realize that your planet is at the very beginning of what has been called the New Age. For hundreds of years this New Age has been hailed as a time with rather a utopian connotation and indeed in my opinion it will approach that at certain points in your history. The light is beginning its penetration so that that

DIAGRAM #15   LEVELS

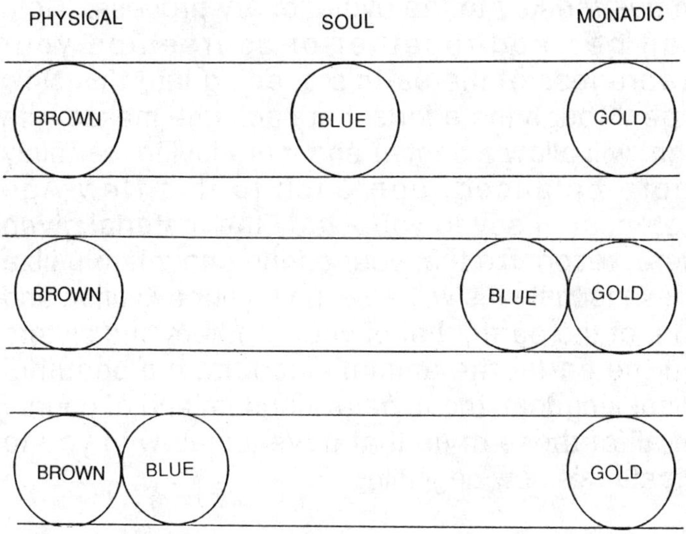

PHYSICAL	SOUL	MONADIC
BROWN	BLUE	GOLD

BROWN		BLUE	GOLD

BROWN	BLUE		GOLD

perspective that you call utopian can be present. It must, however, soften certain resistance patterns first. Some of them are already softer, less crystallized. The light work that you do in 1988 will make a comprehensive difference in what sort of a toehold the New Age can manifest now on the earth. It truly is extremely important to utilize light technology now. It probably is the single most important technique besides channeling which I find is the key to the evolutionary process. Both can be used together of course and your awareness of the earth's opening into this New Age through the efforts that each one makes with light will allow a gentler and more loving, certainly more balanced, approach to this New Age potential. I say to you, study the material given here, recognize that your caring enough to utilize these techniques will allow both your evolution and that of the earth, that of your brothers and sisters on the earth, the animal kingdom, the beautiful plant kingdom, the mineral kingdom and of course of all of those of us that have joined with you to create this new beginning.

USING THE SOUL TO BALANCE THE PHYSICAL AND MONADIC

Sense a stream, a flow of light energy and there are three points within that flow. The Diagram #15 shows you the flow, the stream and the positioning of the three points. One is the physical, the second is the soul and the third is the monad. Visualize the physical as a beautiful brown, the soul as a beautiful blue and the monad as a beautiful gold. I would like you to do the following: As you visualize this energy see a golden radiance, a golden flow coming into the blue from the monadic level, and see the beautiful brown radiating to the blue from the other side, in other words, the blue is receiving energy from the brown and the gold. Now the gold has a lot of energy, you can sense the radiance of it, it is very intense. The blue is attempting to balance that now with the brown and the brown is a little different quality of energy. There's a lot more of it, its more solid, it is not as intense but because there is more of it, the blue through its mobile state is able to balance the two energies (gold & brown) that come in at it.

What I mean by its mobile state is the blue moves back and forth, like the clock - the tick-tock - given to you earlier. It moves back and forth; as it goes to the left it receives from the brown, as it ticks to the right it receives from the gold. There is a light contact as it receives from the brown and there is a light contact as it receives from the gold and the rhythm as it comes literally back and forth. There's an integrative process at the point between the tick and the tock, a uniting or coming together of the light, a pause, if you will, as the energy flow adjusts. It must be mobile enough to have that adjustment in the flow.

Now because what we are symbolizing with the blue is the soul level. It is mobile enough and that's why it is so important for you to be utilizing that soul on the physical plane. Its mobility is the vehicle that you need as an adjustment point from the energies that are received through the earth and through that basic monadic level state of being that is Source relating. If you leave out or don't utilize that central point of the soul the intensity comes into the physical, directly into the physical structure because the personality/ego is centered there. There's no energy buffer of the soul to prevent an inappropriately intense penetration into the physical. We could equate it to lying in the sun so long that you get a sunburn because you haven't gradually gotten used to the utilization of the energy. Now that analogy cannot be taken any further because truly many of you damage your physical structure through sunbathing so lets not pursue that analogy except to help you see that if the vehicle that you are using is not yet ready to accept the intensity of the Source itself then you find a vehicle that is and that vehicle is the soul, that's the purpose truly of the soul.

That higher self is a specific that functions and generates a communicative linkage system between the physical level and the Source level. It's the way that the two link together because you are literally growing, learning, evolving, radiating from the monadic level and also growing and radiating from the physical level. What lies in between is the soul that allows you through its mobility to keep progressing or allowing your energies to respond to ever more light of that Source potential.

Now your monadic level is a part of the Source, a light of Sourceness, that does not mean that it has reached its full potential, indeed it will always be growing and learning and getting brighter in its understanding as far as light, but certainly as far as you are concerned, here on the physical plane, it has its act together or has so much light that your physical sun would look very dull indeed in comparison to it. Therefore it has too much light for you to yet absorb all at once. You need a stepladder of awareness or a means of gradually connecting into what that light potential is. Your soul's mobility allows this. Can you see that the soul is simply a flexible point of awareness within the stream of light that you are? And it can connect what is physical with the basic point of generative magnetic flow.

This is important and this exercise of seeing a clearer light come forth each time the tick and the tock, both exercises, the one given previously and this one, can show you why there is a basic rhythm within existence at all. It allows the light to remain a balanced and yet penetrative tool of evolution without penetrating too much or without guidance. The guidance system that the soul brings is acting as its buffer agent. Indeed the soul is that higher part of your awareness coming to the earth now to guide you in allowing ever more light to be recognized by you, to have it enter the physical structure but to guide you in how much you are ready to use in a balanced manner without damaging the vehicle. Keeping the vehicle in good operating order is appropriate. The soul level will allow that guidance which is needed when you perhaps are so eager for that Source level contact that you don't really recognize you've been burned until after it occurs. Go through that soul level, don't skip over it. It is that point which can teach you the next appropriate step for you. Another word for soul is "guidance system". It is there and important for you now.

ELECTRICAL STIMULATION OF INTEGRATION

See a large circle before you. It is horizontal. You are sitting just outside the circle. You could sit within it but you are not. There are ten vertical pillars placed within the circle, wherever you wish to see them, they are silver metal cylinders, electrical in nature. Sense this is an electrical stimulative point within the circle and the circle simply represents a whole point of view whether it is your whole life, the Source's whole existence, a day that is a whole perspective in your life, a book that has been written that is complete; anything that is complete at a level, the circle represents. So it really represents a coming together, an integration of a particular perspective.

Now create through your third eye a beam of light and have it focus on the whole circle. It will connect into the ten silver rods and you will begin to sense the energy that is being stored within them. Energize them until you know they are very vibrant indeed. It will probably take again around two minutes. Now, this energy is very vibrant, it does not destroy, it simply stimulates. I want you now to go into the circle, become the right size for what you've visualized so that you can move easily among these cylinders touching one and then swinging to another. As you let go of one you grab hold of another, there is a way of continuing to hold on to one and then grasping another as you let go of the first one. Now you can continue to move from one to the other until you have covered all ten of them and then you can go through them again. There is no need to stop your flow and as you move from one to the other you are energized by them. It might equate to a mild electric shock but it is simply stimulative and each one is stimulating you in a little different way.

Now as you move from one to the other, sense that each one prods your consciousness a little, prods the mental processes so that you can think more clearly, prods your spiritual knowingness so that you can connect more completely, prods your emotional body so that you can flow more completely and prods your physical responses so they may respond more completely. Sense then the stimulation as you swing from rod to rod. Do this for three or four moments then you may need to go back and energize the rods again for another minute or two after which you can go back and move again among the rods.

Now this is an integrative exercise, allowing stimulus but movement, allowing movement but balance, allowing balance but the ability to progress a connection through stimulation. In this manner we begin to see, literally, the integrative possibilities of all of what, up until this point, seems stuck into the third dimension, seems crystallized into the third dimension, seems resistive within the third dimension. We begin then to dimensionalize in a way that we haven't recognized before - the physical experience - we can direct a consistent relationship with the dimensions through such an exercise. You can allow the four bodies to really gain a perspective of all of the available physical dimensions in this regard.

As we discussed earlier, sometimes the difficulty on the physical plane is that certain dimensions have been skipped over by certain parts of your consciousness. Through this exercise of stimulation of all ten points you are really entering the third, fourth, and fifth with some reflection of the sixth dimension and allowing a progressive lighting up which releases in rather an intricate way certain resistive points to the use of some of the dimensional focuses. You know you can't always see by certain exercises why I've chosen them or what is being accomplished but this one, again, is very good to allow a complete flowing dimensionally as the points of contact are made that bridge any particular gaps in a dimensional understanding. And that's what many of you have is the gaps or the cracks both, you get caught in the cracks and the gaps are something you have difficulty bridging, it can be either or both and thus you need to begin to sort out the means to allow the four body system to express in the full dimensional experience. The light flows of course on all dimensional levels thus the bridge is the light which then allows your energy to cross it easily and without resistance. It allows then you to be aware of the continuity of the flow, of the integrative possibilities of your life.

ABOUT THE AUTHOR

Janet McClure is a dedicated, committed and loving being who channels many spiritual teachers with extraordinary clarity.

Her channeling career began after she had been studying intensively with the Brotherhood of the White Temple, from which correspondence college she received a Doctor of Metaphysics, and dedicated herself to the service of the Cosmic Plan.

She had been working in business areas while studying metaphysics. Her life changed 180 degrees when she was approached by Djwhal Khul through her intuition and was asked to be a channel for him. Djwhal had been asked by Sanat Kumara (his teacher and the planetary Logos) to return to his earth contacts and aid humanity as he had done when he channeled the information to Alice Bailey 40 years earlier. Djwhal set about making a choice of who to come through and saw that Janet had extensive channeling experience in previous lives and had taught channeling in Egypt. He knew that channeling would come rather easily to her.

Janet was not the first one he approached but she was the first to accept - very enthusiastically accepted. Vywamus says that many are asked to serve but few respond due to not hearing or feeling that certain responsibilities in their lives have yet to be met.

The spiritual teachers were also looking for group strengths and Janet was part of a dedicated group that already had the beginning of the belief structure work. Lillian Harben and the spiritual teacher Thoth were already involved in the group which had developed a specific method to clear blocks that was the foundation of the method that the Tibetan Foundation now uses.

With Janet as the president, the Tibetan Foundation was started in 1982 and was incorporated in January 1983 -- its purpose is to disseminate the teachings of the Spiritual Masters. Since then the organization has grown expansively and Janet has traveled to many parts of the United States, Canada and Europe giving lectures and seminars. Many channels have been trained and are also bringing the spiritual teachers' information and energy to all parts of the country.

The workshops that Janet channels are remarkable in their variety and depth and move participants forward rapidly in their evolution, spiraling them into the New Age. Lately more sound and mantra have been included, giving the workshops new dimensions. She has also generated through her channel an impressive quantity of spiritual information which is published in the form of transcripts and booklets in addition to books such as you are now reading. Her books have been published in the United States and in Europe.

Janet says of her own evolution, "The benefits to me of channeling in terms of clearing blocked areas for myself have been enormous. My evolution is accelerated a great deal through the channeling process. That is one reason why Vywamus chose to train channels because he believes it to be the single most important step you can take to forward your evolution."

7 EXPLORER RACE: THE COUNCIL OF CREATORS

The 13 core members of the Council of Creators discuss their adventures in coming to awareness of themselves and their journeys on the way to the Council on this level. They discuss the advice and oversight they offer to all creators, including the creator of this local universe. These beings are wise, witty and joyous, and their stories of Love's Creation creates an expansion of our concepts as we realize that we live in an expanded, multiple-level reality.

8 EXPLORER RACE and ISIS

Isis, the archetype/prototype of Goddess/Priestess/Feminine Teacher, tells the story of the student she inspired to create the first mystery school in Egypt, and about the confusion between who and what Isis is and the human life of her student, which has enriched our mythology ever since. Isis has never had a human life, but she has guided our Creator in this Explorer Race adventure and has guided and inspired many individual humans both on this planet and other planets, including Orion. The colorful, loving stories she shares will hold you spellbound.

9 EXPLORER RACE and JESUS

The immortal personality who lived the life we know as Jesus, along with his students and friends, describes with clarity and love his life and teaching on Earth 2000 years ago. What has been written or spoken about his life is not disputed or discussed, but these beings lovingly offer their experiences of the events that happened then and of Jesus' time-traveling adventures, because the being known as Jesus had full consciousness. So heartwarming and interesting you won't want to put it down.

10 EXPLORER RACE: EARTH HISTORY AND LOST CIVILIZATIONS EXPLAINED

Zoosh reveals that our planet Earth did not originate in this solar system, but the water planet we live on was brought here from Sirius 65 million years ago. Anomalous archaeological finds and the various ET cultures who founded what we now call lost civilizations are explained with such storytelling skill by Speaks of Many Truths that you feel you were there!

11 EXPLORER RACE: THE ULTIMATE UFO BOOK

This is a UFO book with a twist. The beings who channeled through Robert are the ET beings who were on the ships with humans in the famous case files—Betty and Barney Hill, Betty Andreasson, Travis Walton and many, many others. Here is a completely different perspective on the reality of off-planet/Earth-human interactions. As the various beings describe who they are, your understanding of our neighbors in space will expand.

12 EXPLORER RACE and THE FUTURE-ANCHORED TIME LINE

The past-oriented time line that we are living on now comes to an end in 2012, and this book shows us how to gently and easily step off the old past-oriented path, which ends with the end of the third-dimensional focus, and step onto the new positive, future-oriented time line that leads onward to the fourth dimension and freedom.

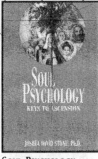

A BEGINNER'S GUIDE TO THE PATH OF ASCENSION
This volume covers the basics of ascension clearly and completely, from the spiritual hierarchy to the angels and star beings.
ISBN 1-891824-02-3

GOLDEN KEYS TO ASCENSION AND HEALING — REVELATIONS OF SAI BABA AND THE ASCENDED MASTERS
This book represents the wisdom of the ascended masters condensed into concise keys that serve as a spiritual guide. These 420 golden keys present the multitude of insights Dr. Stone has gleaned from his own background and his path to God realization.
ISBN 1-891824-03-1

MANUAL FOR PLANETARY LEADERSHIP
Here at last is an indispensable book that has been urgently needed in these uncertain times. It lays out the guidelines for leadership in the world and in one's life. It serves as a reference manual for moral and spiritual living.
ISBN 1-891824-05-8

YOUR ASCENSION MISSION — EMBRACING YOUR PUZZLE PIECE
This book shows how each person's puzzle piece is just as vital and necessary as any other. All aspects of living the fullest expression of your individuality.
ISBN 1-891824-09-0

REVELATIONS OF A MELCHIZEDEK INITIATE
Dr. Stone's spiritual autobiography, beginning with his ascension initiation and progression into the 12th initiation. Filled with insight, tools and information.
ISBN 1-891824-10-4

HOW TO TEACH ASCENSION CLASSES
This book serves as an ideal foundation for teaching ascension classes and presenting workshops. It covers an entire one- to two-year program of classes.
ISBN 1-891824-15-5

$14 95 EACH

ASCENSION AND ROMANTIC RELATIONSHIPS
Inspired by Djwhal Khul, Dr. Stone has written a unique book about relationships from the perspective of the soul and monad rather than just the personality. This presents a broader picture of the problems and common traps of romantic relationships and offers much deeper advice.
ISBN 1-891824-16-3

Behold A Pale Horse

by William Cooper

"I read while in Naval Intelligence that at least once a year, maybe more, two nuclear submarines meet beneath the polar icecap and mate together at an airlock.

Representatives of the Soviet Union meet with the Policy Committee of the Bilderberg Group. The Russians are given the script for their next performance. Items on the agenda include the combined efforts in the secret space program governing Alternative 3.

I now have in my possession official NASA photographs of a moon base in the crater Copernicus."

— Excerpt from pg. 94, BEHOLD A PALE HORSE

$25⁰⁰

Soft cover 500pgs
ISBN 0-929385-22-5

ABOUT THE AUTHOR

Bill Cooper, former United States Naval Intelligence Briefing Team member, reveals information that remains hidden from the public eye. This information has been kept in top-secret government files since the 1940s.

In 1988 Bill decided to "talk" due to events then taking place worldwide. Since Bill has been "talking," he has correctly predicted the lowering of the Iron Curtain, the fall of the Berlin Wall and the invasion of Panama, all of recorded well before the events occurred. His information comes from top-secret documents that he read while with the Intelligence Briefing Team and from over 17 years of thorough research.

Table of Contents
1. Silent Weapons for Quiet Wars
2. Secret Societies and the New World Order
3. Oath of Initiation of an Unidentified Secret Order
4. Secret Treaty of Verona
5. Goodbye USA, Hello New World Order
6. H.R. 4079 and FEMA (Federal Emergency Management Agency)
7. Anti-Drug Abuse Act of 1988 H.R. 5210, P.L. 100-690
8. Are the Sheep Ready to Shear?
9. Anatomy of an Alliance
10. Lessons from Lithuania
11. Coup de Grace
12. The Secret Government
13. Treason in High Places
14. A Proposed Constitutional Model for the Newstates of America
15. Protocols of the Elders of Zion
16. The Story of Jonathan May
17. Documentation: U.S. Army Intelligence Connection with Satanic Church
Appendix A   William Cooper's Military Service Record
Appendix B   UFOs and Area 51
Appendix C   Alien Implants
Appendix D   AIDS
Appendix E   New World Order

LIGHT Technology PUBLISHING

Available from your favorite bookstore or:
LIGHT TECHNOLOGY PUBLISHING
P.O. Box 3540 • Flagstaff, AZ 86003
(520) 526-1345 • (800) 450-0985
FAX (520) 714-1132

Use our on-line bookstore: www.lighttechnology.com

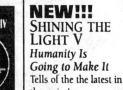